# JOHN WAYNE

John Wayne as Ethan Edwards in *The Searchers* (1956), arguably his best performance. With him, Olive Carey as Mrs. Jorgensen. *The Museum of Modern Art/Film Stills Archive.*

# JOHN WAYNE
# A Bio-Bibliography

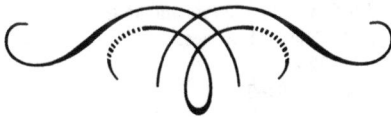

## Judith M. Riggin

Popular Culture Bio-Bibliographies
M. Thomas Inge, Series Editor

Greenwood Press
New York • Westport, Connecticut • London

**Library of Congress Cataloging-in-Publication Data**

Riggin, Judith M.
    John Wayne : a bio-bibliography / Judith M. Riggin.
       p.  cm.—(Popular culture bio-bibliographies, ISSN
  0193-6891)
     Includes index.
     "John Wayne filmography"
     ISBN 0-313-22308-4 (alk. paper)
      1. Wayne, John, 1907-1979.  2. Wayne, John, 1907-1979—
  Bibliography.  3. Motion picture actors and actresses—United
  States—Biography.  I. Title.  II. Series.
  PN2287.W454R54  1992
  791.43'082'092–dc20      91-35218
  [B]

British Library Cataloguing in Publication Data is available.

Copyright © 1992 by Judith M. Riggin

All rights reserved. No portion of this book may be
reproduced, by any process or technique, without the
express written consent of the publisher.

Library of Congress Catalog Card Number: 91-35218
ISBN: 0-313-22308-4
ISSN: 0193-6891

First published in 1992

Greenwood Press, 88 Post Road West, Westport, CT 06881
An imprint of Greenwood Publishing Group., Inc.

(∞)™

The paper used in this book complies with the
Permanent Paper Standard issued by the National
Information Standards Organization (Z39.48-1984).

P

# CONTENTS

# PREFACE

Early in my research for this project, I was reminded by my
mother that my uncle Bob had worked on film crews for Wayne
films in the 1930's and 1940's. Having moved to Arizona for his
health, my uncle hired on as a carpenter for John Ford production
crews working on films in Monument Valley, starting with
*Stagecoach*. I wrote to him, asking for his memories of Wayne.
None of his memories were pleasant. He wrote:

> I worked on several pictures of his, but he never mingled
> with the crew. It was strictly work for him. He never visited,
> only with his close friends, who were part of the cast. . . .
> He never came out at night—only once that I remember, he
> played poker for about an hour in the rec. hall with some of
> his friends and was losing and jumped up and stomped out
> mad. He always had a Mexican girlfriend to stay with unless
> some of his family was there, and I don't remember anyone
> except his son . . . [who] was only nine or ten years old
> then. . . . I guess you can tell I didn't think much of John
> Wayne.

I've pondered the contradiction between my uncle's memories
and the published accounts of Wayne as a star who never forgot

his beginnings as a prop man and who therefore was friendly to all on a film set. They differ too, with accounts of a Wayne who loved to drink and play cards all night—and with fan magazine stories of a Wayne who was a one-woman man and a good father. Such contradictions pinpoint the difficulties of any study of celebrity—especially of movie stars—in American society. The meaning of a celebrity in culture is constructed by a shifting, elusive interaction between the "real" person, the "famous" person, and the public who regards both. To examine this meaning is to shine a light into a prism; one sees many facets, but the light does not reveal a center—that is, a distinct, unified person who is seen the same way by all. Almost always, splits in points of view appear and what one sees is determined by vantage point and angle. Almost always, as with my uncle's view of John Wayne, contradictions appear to complicate the task of the critic. A film star like Wayne emerges a combination of the fictional man found in his films and publicity and the factual person known through fleeting glimpses of the "real" man. Seldom do the two correspond; as Wayne himself once put it: "I've had the most appealing of lives. I've been lucky enough to portray men against the elements at the same time as there was always someone there to bring me the orange juice."

Yet, over a decade after his death, John Wayne still retains a strongly symbolic meaning in American culture. His name alone evokes an image of unquestioned masculinity, aggressive individualism, and fierce patriotism (and militarism) associated with Americans of the old West and Americans at war. But the private Duke, while a strong individualist and political conservative, lived only in the Hollywood West and never served in the military—except in the movies. What he means to the American public has little to do with a private, "real" Wayne. The interaction of his film roles, his personality, and society's perception of both created a mythic public figure. Wayne somehow became, as his posthumous Congressional medal puts it, "John Wayne—American."

Analytical explanations of the process whereby the Wayne myth was created must address complex issues. My discussions in this book are meant to suggest the complexities involved and to offer bibliographic information to guide further exploration of them. In chapters 1 and 2, I focus on the major elements which construct John Wayne as Americans know him. These include the published versions of his life, itself mythologized; his physical appearance and performing style; his movie roles; and the publicity which shaped his public self. In the *Playboy* interview in chapter 3, that public Wayne seems to speak as a private man. These facets of Wayne overlap, contradict each other, and demand further analysis. The bibliographic materials in chapters 4 and 5 offer many directions for such further study. I expect critics will continue to explore the meaning of Wayne as an American figure in coming years, as the society itself tries to reconcile the contradictions of similar facets of its identity.

My interest in the study of film stars and their public meaning began in a NEH Summer Seminar conducted by Leo Braudy. I thank him for his initial guidance, and thank these colleagues from that seminar who have continued to share my interest in years since: Robert Armour, Gerald Duchovnay, and Wade Jennings. I also am grateful for the help of these teaching colleagues who read the manuscript in early versions: Joseph Horobetz, Noel Sipple, and Jenny N. Sullivan. Also, my thanks to M. Thomas Inge, series editor, for kind assistance and the Wayne comic book references. Finally I thank my mother, Golda M. Riggin, for support, but equally for passing on her heritage as a *real* Westerner, which led me to see the importance of John Wayne in the first place.

# 1

# BIOGRAPHY: AN "AMERICAN" LIFE

Much of John Wayne's life is a matter of public record. That is, his early years, career ups and downs, business dealings, and family matters are reported and retold in decades of coverage by the press and in several biographies. Some biographers, including a wife and lover, have written from intimate knowledge about the man. However, private documents of his life—business files, family accounts, personal records and letters—remain largely inaccessible. Therefore, the biographical account which follows depends on material already in print. Published articles and books about Wayne's life differ in a few details, but provide essentially identical versions. Interestingly, most biographical accounts of Wayne seem to reconstruct his life into almost mythic stories of American achievement and American character. The stages of his personal and professional development read as "stories" of a developing "American" man: finding his destiny when his family migrates West; proving himself in a long apprenticeship to his craft; displaying individual strength by pursuing personal dreams and holding to unpopular beliefs; finding fame and fortune as a self-made professional; embodying the best of male camaraderie and sex appeal and fatherhood; achieving a type of immortality as a symbol of American heroism. In these stories, a private, real man seldom appears. The public, mythic, movie star Wayne dominates; but then, it is this John Wayne who is known and valued in American culture.

John Wayne was born Marion Robert Morrison on May 26, 1907, in Winterset, Iowa, a small town near Des Moines. Little in his origins predicted the life to follow. His father, Clyde (Doc) Morrison, was a drugstore clerk; his mother, Mary Brown Morrison, a former telephone operator.

His father was able to buy his own drugstore in nearby Earlham in 1910, and when Marion was three, the family moved there. The store's success brought comfort and some prosperity to their life. First born Marion was followed by a brother, Robert, in 1912 (somehow the "Robert" of Marion's name then became "Michael").[1] Accounts sketch young Marion as an insecure child, given to running away from home. His parents' disagreements filled the house with tension, and his unexpected younger brother threatened him.[2]

The early years of Wayne's life began to shape his future when Doc Morrison contracted tuberculosis. Prescribed to move to a warmer climate, he sent his wife and sons to Des Moines and went to California. He bought eighty acres of desert land in Palmdale, built a rough four-room house, and sent for the family in 1914. Morrison planned to farm corn in the desert; therefore seven-year-old Marion arrived in California to find a new way of family life. He helped his father clear land and plant crops, lived a relatively spare life without electricity or running water, and walked four miles to school. He shot rattlers and jackrabbits to keep them out of the crops; he rode a horse to town for supplies. Although this rugged life might be seen as molding young Morrison into the Westerner he later portrayed, it lasted only two years. Crops failed, horses had to be sold, the desert baked any profits—and the Morrisons moved to Glendale, a tidy L.A. suburb, in 1916. The real influence of the move from Iowa to California would now emerge. They made movies in Glendale.

Marion Morrison grew up in Glendale. His biographer Maurice Zolotow summarizes this growth in nicely melodramatic terms: "It was in Glendale that the shy, underweight, awkward, frightened, neurotic Marion Michael (or Robert) Morrison began to assume the shape of a man and began to become Duke Morrison, actor, football player, and big man on the Glendale Union High School campus."[3]

Young Marion was fascinated by movies. He watched them being made in the mountains and deserts around Glendale. A job passing out handbills for the local movie house provided him with an unlimited pass, and he saw movies several times a week. He played at film making with his friends.

"Marion" became "Duke" thanks to the men at a firehouse near one of his Glendale homes. (Doc Morrison continued to change jobs and houses, but the family stayed in Glendale.) Marion visited the firemen accompanied by his Airedale, Duke. They called the boy "Duke," too, and the name stuck.

By the time he graduated from high school in 1925, Duke Morrison predicted the man, John Wayne. He was a tall athlete, an academic success, and a leader in his class. Although he aspired to be and was nominated as an alternate to the Naval Academy, a football scholarship drew him to attend the University of Southern California, aiming toward a law degree. He pledged Sigma Chi, played on the freshman Trojan football squad, and made good grades. And the summer after his first year of college, he got a job as a propman on the "swing gang" at Fox Film Studios (thanks to Tom Mix, who found work for USC football players).

This job, in the summer of 1926, put Morrison into the world that would become his life. One early assignment was to herd chickens, ducks, and geese for a scene from *Mother Machree*, being directed by John Ford. He also worked that summer on Ford's *Four Sons* and *Hangman's House*. John Ford would be Wayne's mentor—make him a star and shape his acting talent—and their first work together set the relationship. Both men recounted tales of the work at Fox which show Ford as a testy, challenging authority figure to young Duke Morrison. But he also stood up to Ford's bullying, winning respect and eventually friendship. Wayne repeatedly credited Ford as the single most important influence in his professional life.

Duke Morrison's first appearance is a matter of dispute, but it is certain Ford gave him a small role in *Hangman's House* that summer. He appears on the screen as a rowdy in the crowd at a horse race.

Morrison returned to USC in the fall of 1926, but a series of circumstances ended his college education after that second year and put him back to work for Fox. During the Thanksgiving holidays he met Josephine Saenz, the daughter of a Mexican doctor, and fell in love. He also injured his shoulder body surfing. The injury eventually kept him from playing football and meant the loss of his scholarship. His love for Josie was frustrated by her social position; he could not hope to date let alone marry her without money and a future. Discouraged, he lost interest in school, he drank, and his studies faltered. Although he finished his sophomore year, he had no way to finance two more years. He returned to work for Ford and Fox that summer in 1927, hoping to make enough money for a future with Josie Saenz. He never left film making after that.

The next twelve years, from July 1927 until the release of *Stagecoach* in March 1939, Duke Morrison learned his craft, laboring in a long apprenticeship. He propped, stunted, and appeared in small roles for Fox until 1929. Then Raoul Walsh, unable to get Gary Cooper as lead for an epic Western, pulled him out of the prop room to star in *The Big Trail*. Studio head Winfield Sheehan changed his name to "John Wayne" and signed him to a five-year contract, but the film lost money. Wayne received good reviews, went on publicity tours, but did not become a star. After he made two more Fox films, the studio dropped the option on his contract. Columbia Pictures picked up the option, but Harry Cohn, head of the studio, decided Wayne was fooling around with his actress girlfriend, put him into secondary roles (in one he played a corpse), and dropped his contract.

From this point in 1932, Wayne's career began to build—slowly. He found work on "Poverty Row," the stretch of low-budget film companies, and began to make films—most Westerns—for Mascot, then Warner's, then Monogram-Lone Star, then Republic, then Universal, and finally again Republic.

His first Fox contract had paid him $75 a week. He signed with Mascot for $300 a week and over the next years, as his reputation as a "B" western star increased, his salary rose to $4,000 a picture. And Wayne *did* become a western star. For Mascot (1932–33) he did three adventure serials, and at Warner's (1932–33) he starred in remakes of four Ken Maynard silent westerns and two other original westerns. After four other lesser Warner's roles, he signed with Monogram to make Lone Star westerns (1933–35). He made sixteen, most directed by Robert N. Bradbury, and began a career-long association with stunt man Yakima Canutt. With Canutt, he developed a choreographed fight technique notably realistic in contrast to the careless knockabout style of other western actors. Lone Star also cast Wayne as the first singing cowboy, dubbing his voice as "Singin' Sandy" in *Riders of Destiny*. Monogram merged with other small companies to form Republic Studios, and Wayne galloped through eight more "B" westerns until 1936. Then, tired of westerns, he signed with Universal for a six-picture series of undistinguished sports and adventure films. When these roles did not alter his status as actor, he returned to Republic (1938–39) for a final series of westerns as one of "The Three Mesquiteers." George Sherman directed him in these eight films. (Four of the series were released after *Stagecoach* in 1939.) Thus John Wayne acted in forty-four westerns during this twelve-year period (and twenty-five other films, three of which were twelve-episode serials). He became known as a staple of action Westerns—a hero of pure virtue, stout heart, strong fist, and white hat. He increased his income but his acting range remained limited,[4] and he was not a Hollywood star. John Ford made him both actor and star in 1939 when he directed him in *Stagecoach*.

Wayne had realized one goal during these years. He felt secure enough in his income by 1933 to marry Josephine Saenz. And his growing family—Michael in 1934, Antonia in 1936, Patrick in 1937, and Melinda in 1939—required the continual labors for their support. Unfortunately, the work also took its toll on the marriage.

During the apprenticeship years making B's, Wayne put in long
work hours away from his wife and small children. Also, because
of a growing friendship with John Ford and other men who
formed a circle of hard-drinking, fighting, gambling, boating
buddies, Wayne moved away from his wife's companionship.
These factors, along with fundamental differences in tastes and
values, strained the Wayne marriage. The pressure of stardom
and work that followed *Stagecoach* cracked the union. A devout
Catholic, Josie Wayne was reluctant to divorce but by the early
forties, the two in essence lived apart. In 1941, Wayne met a
Mexican actress, Esperanza Baur, in Mexico City. Smitten, he
invited her to come to Hollywood in 1943 to join him and further
her career. Their open affair prompted Josie Wayne to file for
legal separation in 1943; the divorce was final December 26,
1945. Wayne married Esperanza (nicknamed "Chata") Baur
January 18, 1946.

Although the early forties brought personal problems, they
marked emergence into stardom. Wayne's fame as a box office
hero and Hollywood personality grew rapidly after *Stagecoach*.
Most reviewers loved the film, and it gathered a best-picture
Academy Award nomination. *Stagecoach* lost out to *Gone With
the Wind*, but John Ford won the best director Oscar for his work.
Wayne's reputation gained from the critical acceptance of the film,
even though his performance was not singularly praised. And the
public took a liking to him. Capitalizing on this new appeal, RKO
and Republic, the studios still holding his contracts, quickly put
him into "A" features—adventure films that restated his *Stagecoach* image in varying styles. In RKO's *Allegheny Uprising*
(1939) he is a colonial rebel; Claire Trevor, his *Stagecoach*
co-star, pursues him as a spunky heroine. Wayne and Trevor are
paired again in a drama of pre-Civil War Kansas, *The Dark
Command* (1940). Also in 1940, he leads immigrants west in
*Three Faces West*, is O'Neill's naive Swedish sailor in Ford's *The
Long Voyage Home*, and wins over Marlene Dietrich's chanteuse
in *Seven Sinners*. Off and running, Wayne's career hit stride
through the forties. The range of his roles expanded, the budget

and scope of productions grew, and the importance of the directors and co-stars matched his growing box office appeal. Including those above, thirty-three Wayne films were released during this decade; in them, typically Wayne is a man of action and a romantic lead. A list of films and leading ladies reflects the variety. In 1941: *A Man Betrayed* with Frances Dee, *Lady From Louisiana* with Ona Munson, *The Shepherd of the Hills* with Betty Field. In 1942: *Lady for a Night* with Joan Blondell, *Reap the Wild Wind* with Paulette Goddard, *The Spoilers* with Dietrich, *In Old California* with Binnie Barnes, *Flying Tigers* with Anna Lee, *Reunion in France* with Joan Crawford, and *Pittsburgh* with Dietrich. In 1943: *A Lady Takes a Chance* with Jean Arthur, *In Old Oklahoma* with Martha Scott. In 1944: *The Fighting Seabees* with Susan Hayward, *Tall in the Saddle* with Ella Raines. In 1945: *Flame of the Barbary Coast* with Ann Dvorak, *Back to Bataan*, *They Were Expendable* with Donna Reed, *Dakota* with Vera Ralston. In 1946: *Without Reservations* with Claudette Colbert. In 1947: *Angel and the Badman* with Gail Russell, *Tycoon* with Laraine Day. Also, as this decade of hard work came to a close, Wayne had acted for many important directors: Raoul Walsh, Ford, Tay Garnett, Henry Hathaway, Cecil B. DeMille, Jules Dassin, William Seiter, Edward Dmytryk, and Mervyn LeRoy.

This list of films outlines Wayne's growing fame and power. As a new star in 1942, he was working hard; seven films were released that year. Soon, however, his popularity at the box office meant he could deal to make fewer films for more money. In each succeeding year up to 1948, only a few Wayne films appeared. The difference between seven and one or two films a year reflects the contract he negotiated with Republic in 1946. It gave him ten percent of the gross against a $150,000 salary. More important, it limited his work for Republic to one high-budget film a year and allowed him the freedom to work for other studios and produce his own films. He was gaining economic power unusual in Hollywood then and making big money.

This list of forties films also reveals—in hindsight—few first rate performances. None of the films, even the two done with

John Ford (*The Long Voyage Home* and *They Were Expendable*), shows Wayne to be an accomplished actor. They demonstrate the progression of Wayne's career, but not progressive development as an actor. However, another flurry of films in 1948 and 1949 changed this, pushing Wayne into a new stage in his career. In 1948 came two landmark films, *Fort Apache* for John Ford and *Red River* for Howard Hawks. The performances in these films mark the emergence of Wayne as an actor—not just a star—to be reckoned with. Both directors call upon him to play mature characters whose personalities resonate age and complexity. For his Tom Dunson in *Red River*, Wayne seems particularly to pull together fragments of rage, strength, obsession, and pain that are only glimpsed in earlier performances. These maturing roles led to others. Although three rather ordinary vehicles—*Three God-fathers* for Ford, *Wake of the Red Witch*, and *The Fighting Kentuckian*—followed in 1949, so did *She Wore A Yellow Ribbon* (Ford again) and *Sands of Iwo Jima*. In the former, Wayne plays a grand old man of the cavalry, Nathan Brittles. Many felt this to be an Oscar-winning performance, but Wayne was not nominated for it. Instead, he received a nomination in 1949 for his bitter-sweet playing of Marine Sergeant John Stryker. The industry acknowledged growth in his craft, but he didn't win. He wouldn't win for twenty more years. Thus, if the first decade of Wayne's work marked time as an apprenticeship, the next brought out the master craftsman. By 1950, Wayne's power and reputation as a figure in Hollywood and American culture was made. Over the ensuing thirty-some years, the shape of his career would alter, but never decline. His stature as a cultural figure would increase.

The tough guy of most of the forties films, especially the Westerns and war movies, shaped Wayne's cultural image. He had been a cowboy star for years already, but a series of military roles in *Flying Tigers, Reunion in France, Operation Pacific, The Fighting Seabees, Back to Bataan, They Were Expendable, Without Reservations*, and notably *Sands of Iwo Jima* identified him with America's fighting spirit and patriotism. This image became so set in the American consciousness that eventually the

Army and Marines cautioned their trainees *not* to attempt fool-hardy "John Wayne" heroics. Wayne himself was too old and too much a father to serve in World War II. Instead, he toured installations and visited the troops. Evidently he regretted not being a warrior; a Ford anecdote tells of Wayne having to leave a meeting of those involved in *They Were Expendable* in tears because he was ashamed to be among men who had served with distinction—Ford, Robert Montgomery, writer "Spig" Wead—while he made movies.[5] Ironically, of course, his war films placed Wayne in the public memory as the archetypal "gung-ho" American fighting man.

Another aspect of Wayne's image in American culture appeared in the late forties—an involvement in conservative political activities. In February 1944, several hundred film industry people met to organize the Motion Picture Alliance for the Preservation of American Ideals. In a Hollywood community bristling with political conflicts, this group ran counter to somewhat prevalent liberal attitudes. Feverishly anticommunist and patriotic, the Alliance was also accused of reactionary and anti-Semitic politics. Whatever the truth of such accusations may be, it is clear that the Alliance's vow to "fight" communist infiltration of motion pictures industries colored the witch-hunting atmosphere of the hearings of the House Committee on Un-American Activities in the late forties. In 1949, Wayne was elected to what would be the first of three terms as president of this group. Throughout the forties and fifties, although he never testified against any Hollywood figures in the HUAC hearings, Wayne remained an outspoken anticommunist. His work with the Alliance reflects this, and his public statements of his views, linked to his screen image as an American military or western hero, set him in the public imagination as the embodiment of conservative, "traditional" American values.

However, once again, private problems accompanied public achievement for Wayne. His second marriage ended early in the fifties, this time in scandal. Chata was a lively but difficult mate;

heavy drinking and fights, spiced by the presence of Chata's
mother who moved in during the first year of the marriage,
became the pattern. Wayne's work absences, drinking, and temper
contributed. By 1953, the union had soured completely. Chata
filed for divorce, and the couple could not arrive at a settlement
agreement. Forced into court, the divorce went to trial in November 1953. The testimony filled the papers with show biz scandal,
and this publicity led to a bitter out-of-court settlement. However,
Wayne's difficulties didn't forestall another marriage.

In 1951, Wayne had met Peruvian actress Pilar Palette on a trip
to South America. Soon after divorced, she came to test in
Hollywood the following year. They met again, began to date,
and married the day Wayne's divorce became final, November 1,
1954, in Hawaii where he was completing *The Sea Chase*. (Chata
Baur Wayne died of a heart attack, presumably aggravated by
alcoholism, within a year.)

Wayne's marriage to Pilar Palette would prove a somewhat
happier one. They had three children, Aissa (1956), Ethan
(1962), and Marissa (1966), and she seemed to adjust more easily
to Wayne as an often-absent, work-obsessed husband. Ultimately,
however, even their marriage felt the strain. After nearly twenty
years, they were separated in 1973. Wayne seems to have
remained, in spite of this history of marital difficulties, a family
man. His children figured in his life, often visiting him on location
and spending vacations with him. The oldest son Michael eventually came to run Wayne's production company in the sixties;
son Patrick, the actor, appeared in many films with his father.
The three youngest also appeared with Wayne as his children or
grandchildren in films during the sixties and seventies.

During the fifties, Wayne's career reflects his growing power
as a Hollywood businessman. His renegotiated contract with
Republic had stipulated he could produce films. His first production was *Angel and the Badman* in 1947. Others followed and he
joined with Robert Fellows in 1951 to form the Wayne-Fellows
Production Company. (Their first film, *Big Jim McLain* in 1952,
reflects the anticommunist politics Wayne was involved in. Cast

as a HUAC investigator, Wayne battles communist spies and insurgents in Hawaii.) The production company, later renamed Batjac Productions after the name of a trading company in *Reap the Wild Wind*, produced fourteen films during the fifties, six starring Wayne. While none was a classic, all made money. During this period, Wayne's business interests expanded beyond movie making. In 1941 he had hired Bō Roös as his business manager. Over the years, Roös channeled Wayne's profits into private investments and real estate, the best known his huge cattle and cotton ranch near Stanfield, Arizona.

But all the projects were ultimately fed by the large sums Wayne commanded as an actor. A Wayne picture usually meant profit for all concerned. Beginning in 1949, Wayne was voted among the "Top Ten Stars" by movie theater exhibitors for each of the next twenty-four years (excluding 1958). He was number one on the list in 1950, 1951, 1954, and 1971. Such a rating shows that his work guaranteed box office profits; similar polls reflect the same standing. That profitability meant that Wayne was able to demand commensurate salaries. In 1956, for example, he struck a contract deal with 20th Century-Fox that made him the highest paid actor in Hollywood to date: two million dollars for three pictures.

During the fifties, Wayne also added to his reputation as an actor. Having broken into more mature, complex roles in the late forties, he went on to make twenty-five films during the next decade, up to 1960. These films are a mixed lot, but a handful represent the best work of his career. Those which might be counted as routine Wayne vehicles are *Operation Pacific* (1951), *Flying Leathernecks* (1951), *Big Jim McLain* (1952), *Trouble Along the Way* (a rather untypical domestic melodrama–1953), *Island in the Sky* (1953), *The High and the Mighty* (1954), *The Sea Chase* (1955), *Blood Alley* (1955), *The Wings of Eagles* (1957), and *Legend of the Lost* (1957). These roles play variations on Wayne's typical strong, stubborn hero who overcomes physical danger and troublesome women. Three other films are unusual failures: *The Conqueror* (1956) and *Jet Pilot* (1957), produced by Howard Hughes at RKO, and *The Barbarian and the Geisha* (1958). *The Conqueror* deserves its reputation as a delightfully bad movie, but Wayne's work as Genghis Khan cannot be singled out for blame. The writing and direction victimize all the performers. In *Jet Pilot*, Wayne performs as his standard romantic tough guy, but the rather bizarre erotic tone (reinforced by the sequences of aerial mating dances between jet fighters) makes the film laughable. And under John Huston's direction in *The Barbarian and the Geisha*, Wayne is both cast and acts ineffectively against type. His soft-talking diplomat gets trapped in a brawling body, and an erratic performance results.

In a group of other films, however, Wayne extends his acting skills: *The Quiet Man* (1952), *Hondo* (1953), *The Searchers* (1956), *Rio Bravo* (1959), and *The Horse Soldiers* (1959). John Ford directed Wayne in *The Quiet Man*, *The Searchers*, and *The Horse Soldiers*, and Howard Hawks directed him in *Rio Bravo*. Thus Wayne again is brought to his best by these directors, as he was in the late forties. The chemistry of such combinations is hard to analyze, but strong directors with complete control of the film seem also to control and elicit Wayne's best acting. All these performances temper the standard Wayne hero. Subtle delivery and gesture either soften or rigidify his brash physicality. Also, these films scan as a continued movement to roles of older, even aging heroes. As the man aged, the actor (and some directors) capitalized on the fallible strength and wisdom that aging could add to characterization. In general, Wayne's films of the fifties extended the work that came before: his familiar heroic character guaranteed big box office profits and provided a basis for increasingly accomplished acting.

By 1960, the Duke was a giant in the business, drawing big salaries, producing his own films, and creating memorable roles. His financial investments were wide-ranging and generally profitable. In 1959 and 1960, Wayne worked on a long beloved project that ultimately tied up his energies as producer, director, and actor; endangered his professional reputation; and exhausted his personal fortune. This was the multimillion dollar production of

*The Alamo*. For over ten years, Wayne had been trying to arrange financing for a film version of the last stand at the Alamo. Deals he made with Republic and Warner Brothers never came together, and when Wayne contracted with United Artists in 1958, he made their partial financing of the project part of the arrangements. Ultimately, Wayne's insistence on the scale and detail of the production ran the costs to well over six-and-a-half million dollars. Batjac was mortgaged, and Wayne's private funds had to make up the millions of dollars overrun.

Money didn't buy quality, however. Wayne's creative touch was too heavy. He played a second lead as Davy Crockett and directed the film broadly to emphasize patriotic sentimentality and lively battle action. He also approved a publicity campaign that equated the film with the event—and with the 1960 presidential election—in importance. The conservative jingoism of the publicity campaign did the film little service, either. Although relatively popular at the box office, the film lost money, and only rereleases and television broadcasts enabled United Artists to recover its investment. In the industry, the craft of *The Alamo* (and Wayne's influence) earned twelve Academy Award nominations, including Best Picture. Some overly zealous campaigning for Oscar votes (mostly by Chill Wills who wanted the Best Supporting Actor Award) darkened the film's chances, however, and it won only for Best Sound Achievement. Perhaps *The Alamo* can be interpreted as an illustration of Wayne's willingness to put his all into something he believed in; perhaps it shows a lack of artistic judgment and perspective. Whatever the case, Wayne's dedication led to disappointment that the film wasn't a success and to debts that pushed him into a new period of energetic, high-paid movie making.

Over the next fifteen years, until his last movie in 1976, Wayne made twenty-eight films—and he made money doing it. Following *The Alamo*, Wayne finished up work for a lucrative contract he'd made with 20th Century-Fox back in the fifties, and then signed with Paramount for ten pictures. Although his customary fee was now $750,000 a picture, he signed for $600,000 each for the ten because Paramount would pay off the contract in a cash-on-the-line advance, allowing Wayne to eliminate many debts from *The Alamo* (and some other bad investments). Soon after, he asked and got over $200,000 for a cameo appearance in Darryl Zanuck's *The Longest Day*. And by the late sixties, he could demand $100,000 for a film plus thirty-five percent of the profits. Also, the films he made for Batjac were strong at the box office, making him more money.

But Wayne was working hard for his money, and he was adding more range to his acting along the way. For instance, six Wayne films were released during 1960, 1961, and 1962. Two are cameo appearances in *The Longest Day* (1962) and *How the West Was Won* (1962), but the others represent the directions his work would take from then on. In *North to Alaska* (1960), Wayne handles rough-and-tumble comedy well, showing a tendency to make fun of his own bravado. The same style flavors his performances in *Hatari!* (1962), *Donovan's Reef* (1963), *McLintock!* (1963), and, of course, *True Grit* (1969) and *Rooster Cogburn* (1975). *The Comancheros* (1961) is a rather mediocre, standard Wayne western, strong on action and a certain wry maturity. He made many films like it (not all Westerns): *Circus World* (1964), *The Sons of Katie Elder* (1965), *The War Wagon* (1967), *The Hellfighters* (1968), *The Undefeated* (1969), *Chisum* (1970), *Rio Lobo* (1970), *Big Jake* (1971), *The Cowboys* (1972), *The Train Robbers* (1973), *Cahill, U.S. Marshall* (1973), *McQ* (1974), and *Brannigan* (1975). Sprinkled through these years of profitable if not remarkable performances are, again, a few that rise above. *The Man Who Shot Liberty Valance* (1962) reworks the Wayne hero as a poignant, fading figure. This quality enriches also his performances in *In Harm's Way* (1965), *El Dorado* (1967), *True Grit* (1969), and *The Shootist* (1976). In these, Wayne as character and as performer converge into engaging portraits of men who have matured beyond heroics. And the achievement of Wayne's acting—over thirty years of notable performances—was finally acknowledged by his peers with the Oscar for Best Actor he won in 1969 for *True Grit*.

The Oscar marked the end of a difficult period in Wayne's career, however—one in which his politics and public image threatened to eclipse his screen work. His name had become synonymous with blind, hawkish conservatism. During the sixties, Wayne became an increasingly outspoken defender of the war in Vietnam and right-wing Americanism in general. He had not strayed from the anticommunist attitudes he backed in the fifties, and the war focused his beliefs. He actively supported Ronald Reagan as a conservative candidate for the governorship of California and was among the first big names to visit the troops in Vietnam, making his first tour in 1966. In 1968, he was invited to address the Republican National Convention in Miami as it set about nominating Richard Nixon for election. Probably most telling in establishing Wayne's public image as war supporter was his second effort at producing, directing, and acting in a film vehicle he chose as a personal project: *The Green Berets* (1968).

This film will probably be reevaluated by critics removed in time, but it is, like *The Alamo*, a bluntly jingoistic film, and the cooperation from the Army in its production raised a controversy. Once again, Wayne persevered with his own vision, and the film (unlike *The Alamo*) was a money-maker, grossing $7,000,000 the first three months. The fuss over *The Green Berets* was followed, however, by the success of *True Grit* and the Oscar, and Wayne's career was rejuvenated. Indeed, as the passion over the U.S. involvement in Vietnam faded in the seventies, the media and the left seemed to be drawn back to Wayne in admiration of the strength of his convictions. He emerged as the noble opposition, even to the extent that he was invited to Harvard in 1974 to confront the student body. He arrived in a tank.

Part of this softening toward Wayne was the result of a "comeback" as an actor. However, his struggles with cancer also drew public admiration and played a significant part in forming the mythic Wayne that moved toward a brave and very public death in the seventies.

This element of Wayne's image became public in 1964 when his cancerous lung was removed. After some initial subterfuge about the reason for hospitalization, Wayne vigorously supported cancer research in advertisements that voice how he "licked the big C," clearly evoking his reputation as a hero who could do in the "bad guys," among them, cancer. Then in what would be his last film, *The Shootist* (1976), he played a gunslinger doomed by "a cancer" to a painful, undignified death. His character chose to go out in a showdown instead. By 1978 this role seemed an eerie coincidence. Wayne underwent heart surgery in March of 1978 and bounced back, responding to an outpouring of fan mail and public attention with statements of his intention to return to work. He did some television work and public appearances. In January 1979, however, gall bladder surgery revealed a cancerous stomach which had to be removed. Jimmy Carter, Queen Elizabeth, and countless Americans responded to the imminent loss of the symbol of American strength and manhood, sending personal wishes for his recovery. Congress hurriedly approved a bill to strike a gold congressional medal honoring "John Wayne—American." Again, he fought back, appearing to the American public and to his peers as a thin, aged figure at the Academy Awards in April 1979 to present the Oscar for the best picture to *Deerhunter*. But Wayne soon reentered the UCLA Medical Center and died—his family around him—on June 11, 1979.

The tributes and obituaries following his death speak repeatedly of the passing of "the last," "one of the few remaining," "the most important." Such phrases are attached to his craft, as he is hailed as one of the great Hollywood stars. They are applied to his personality, as he is lauded for a largeness of body and spirit. But most often, they signify his place in American culture: "the last cowboy," "one of our few remaining symbols of heroism," "the embodiment of those qualities of spirit and character that Americans aspired to and admired," "a folk hero . . . . whose magnitude and emotional conviction took on an enduring symbolic importance," "a private monument to the American way of life," and ultimately, a man who gave all of us "a dream of daring and high spirit."[6] Thus John Wayne's life took on mythic significance through his art. A recounting of the events of his career and personal experience does not adequately explain how this came to be. Clearly, he lived a life marked by hard work, risk taking, and achievement—perhaps an American success story. But the John Wayne whose death is marked by phrases like those quoted is not to be found in personal history; that man is on the screen.

## NOTES

1. Maurice Zolotow, *Shooting Star: A Biography of John Wayne* (New York: Simon and Schuster, 1974; rev. ed. 1979) 5-6. This and subsequent Zolotow citations are from the 1979 Pocket Books paperback.
2. Zolotow 9-11. Zolotow interviewed former neighbors, residents of Earlham who remember Wayne as a boy.
3. Zolotow 18.
4. Allen Eyles, *John Wayne* (New York: A. S. Barnes and Company, 1976; rev. ed. 1979) 27-55. Eyles details the ups and downs of Wayne's acting in the "B's."
5. Zolotow 206-208.
6. These quotes appeared in obituaries and tributes in *The Washington Post* (some syndicated elsewhere): George F. Will, " 'The Last Cowboy,' " 17 June 1979: 37; Tom Shales, "Duke Redux," 14 June 1979: C1; Martin Weil, "The Duke is Dead—John Wayne Succumbs to Cancer," 12 June 1979: A1; Gary Arnold and Kenneth Turan, "The Duke—'More Than Just a Hero,' " 13 June 1979: A1; Eve Zibart, "Everyone's Symbol: 'A Man Who Made His Code and Lived By It,' "13 June 1979: E1; Charles Kuralt on CBS as quoted in Shales C15.

# 2

# IMAGE: AN "AMERICAN" STAR

In January 1974, John Wayne rode through the streets of Cambridge, Massachusetts, atop an eleven-ton armored personnel carrier. He had accepted an invitation from the editors of the *Harvard Lampoon* that dared him to "set foot in the wilderness of Harvard"[1] to receive the *Lampoon*'s Brass Balls award for "machismo" and a "penchant for hitting people in the mouth,"[2] and to premiere his film, *McQ*. His arrival and later meeting with students before the film made him a hit. The students threw snowballs at the personnel carrier and threw taunts at him before the premiere, but he emerged untouched by either. By all accounts, he charmed his audience.

This episode says a great deal about John Wayne's place in American culture. The editors invited him because of his symbolic significance in American society at the time; his outspoken right-wing political views represented one side of a society polarized by the Vietnam War. By this point in his career, Wayne's views also merged with his screen image as a two-fisted hero. Of course, Wayne himself invited such a merging, particularly in film projects like *The Green Berets* (1968). But as a movie star, he brought to this appearance more than his politics. He lived up to its challenge—as an entertainer and celebrity—by acting larger than life for his audience. Wayne's Harvard appearance presented him in a dramatic scene, behaving like a public political figure, like a macho male, and like a movie star, all simultaneously.

And beyond his representative significance in those roles, Wayne's impact at Harvard expresses a less obvious value he seems to offer American culture. He surprised the students with his good humor and willingness to play, even to joke about his own image. He seems always to have been a man able to live with himself—one who has somehow made a whole person of his private and public selves, a satisfying model for many who struggle with the dissonance of modern life. Political and star images aside, he came to be viewed as a uniquely whole, heroic, and "American" man. Through his distinctive appearance and his acting style, through an image created by many film roles and star publicity, and through his own efforts to sustain the image and make it "real," John Wayne came to represent a set of intertwined ideas and a type of manhood and self-assurance linked to a mythic America of the past.

Wayne's representative value in American society begins with the John Wayne that appeared—still appears—in the movies. His impact began with, and is sustained by, his physical appearance and acting. On the screen, he commands attention through his looks, his movement, and his delivery of lines. These elements communicate certain human qualities which transfer to the characters he portrays and thereby to him. Their essence is tension— the tension of power under control and of soft interior concealed by hard exterior.

Wayne's size dominates his appearance. At 6'4" and over 200 pounds, he fills the screen and often towers over other actors. As one critic puts it, "The key to Wayne's acting style lies in his size and strength. Wayne has so much physical power that his presence in any scene dominates the action, even if Wayne is static and silent."[3] His height and weight are well-proportioned, communicating bulk and power.

As he ages, Wayne carries more weight in his middle than on his broad shoulders, and his large face, hands, and arms grow meaty. This description of Wayne in his fifties, observed on the set of *Donovan's Reef*, captures his physical impact:

> He is all bulk, but he moves himself gracefully, like a mean tomcat. His head is large, his beaked nose is large and his beefy hands are large. The skin under his chin is holding up well and makeup obliterates the permanent flush in his cheeks. Just above his belt, he has a paunch, minimized by low-strung trousers. . . . His eyes, heavy-lidded above and deeply lined in the corners, look old but not tired. The well-known, thin-lipped, bedroom grin is apparently the natural set of his mouth since he is almost always wearing it, even when throwing horrendous punches.[4]

At any age, Wayne's powerful body at rest stands with ease, usually with weight on the right leg and arms akimbo. His large body, set in that graceful posture, is an image familiar to thousands. Wayne's facial features are equally familiar: the furrowed brow, the hooded eyes, the lined ruddy cheeks, and the flinty slash of a mouth. (Early snapshots and school photos show the same Wayne; he did not develop a "look" for the movies. Posed for a childhood picture, five-year-old Wayne rests weight on one leg in the familiar stance. A high school football picture taken when he was eighteen reveals a young brow already deeply furrowed by his squint.)

The size, the bulk, the strength, the etched features, and the ease with which Wayne carried all establish him as a figure of power on the screen.

However, physical description alone does not communicate what it is to watch Wayne the performer. His rolling walk, his violent fist-fighting, his brusque embraces, even his alert stillness express physical power under control—often graceful control. The dancer Gene Kelly once chose Wayne as the exemplar of male grace: ". . . Duke moved with the grace of an athlete, and the poise of a man who, knowing his strength, can also show himself to be tender and gentle."[5]

His gestures and facial expressions suggest the same control; small movements communicate a great deal and outbursts release emotions held in check. His angular features form a mask; often only the eyes express motives or feelings of the character. Terry Curtis Fox analyzes the cumulative effect of Wayne's style:

> . . . His acting always had the effect of a mask. You sensed that there was something beneath those multilayered poses, and you had no idea what it was . . . Wayne kept his interior force frighteningly hidden. He could *suggest* a past—through a glance, a turning of the head, a shying away of the body—but he would never *reveal* one. Wayne let you know through his acting, that you could see only as much as he would show.[6]

The other element of Wayne's film presence, besides his appearance and his style of movement, is his speech. His voice is deep, and his delivery slow and rhythmic, punctuated by unexpected pauses and emphases. Joan Didion hears essential manhood in that voice; "When John Wayne spoke, there was no mistaking his intentions; he had a sexual authority so strong that even a child could perceive it."[7] Overall, his vocal qualities are so individual and consistent that they can be instantly recognized—and frequently imitated.

The familiarity of John Wayne's physical appearance and performance style bonds the identity of the actor to the identity of the real man. Many assessments of Wayne's skill as an actor, as well as Wayne's own explanations of his approach to is work, equate the two. In the earlier years of his career, he and others often dismissed his acting accomplishments. A standard claim was that John Wayne didn't act, he just played himself. Director Henry Hathaway, with whom Wayne frequently worked, explained, "There are two kinds of actors. There's the kind that are natural-born-for-what-they-are actors. John Wayne is a natural-born strong man, he just looks, he's strong. . . ."[8] And Wayne himself asserted in 1949, "I don't act, I react. . . . I always play

John Wayne. . . . I'm not an actor and I don't pretend to be one.
All I can do is sell sincerity."[9]
   Later, Wayne and others assessed his ability to "play himself"
or act "natural" in a different way. By 1960, Wayne's explanation
of his "reacting" changed: "What I should have added . . . is that
reacting is a form of acting and damned hard work."[10] Wayne
also maintained,

   Motion pictures are like sitting in a room with someone and
   talking across a table. If you overact, they're quite aware of
   it. If it's your ego and it's a flamboyancy, they accept it and
   have fun with it. But you can't overact in a picture unless it
   is that . . . if there's too much falseness, man, you lose them
   like that. Nobody can *be* natural. To be natural, you'd drop
   a scene.[11]

   On another occasion, his comments are even more explicit: "I
know that the hardest thing to do in a scene is to do nothing, or
seem to do nothing, because doing nothing requires extreme work
and discipline."[12] Colleagues praise such work. Howard Hawks,
director of several of Wayne's westerns, said, "Wayne is under-
rated. He's a much better actor than he's given credit for being."[13]
And British actor Sir Ralph Richardson just before Wayne's death
"remarked in an interview that the 'Duke' projected the kind of
mystery one associated with great acting."[14] In his last interview,
Wayne told Barbara Walters that "I know I'm a good actor. But
it's . . . I've been at it for fifty years. I should have learned
something, you know."[15]
   Critics David Thomson and Terry Curtis Fox both term him a
"great" actor, and Fox elaborates, characterizing Wayne as a
"nineteenth-century iconographic actor whose performances
were totally exterior. . . . [with] artifice so well-developed—and
maintained for such a long and consistent period of time—that it
was seen as behavioral."[16] These evaluations of Wayne as actor
stress the merging of man and screen image. As Wayne refined
his acting technique, he simultaneously defined his persona as a

man. Performance became the person; ". . . his great feat was
not to play 'himself,' whatever that means, but to fashion a new
self from his screen image."17

Thus, the given of John Wayne on the screen—his body, face,
actions, voice—has a residual and continuing power. On screen,
he communicates physical strength which implies strength of
character; that strength is carried with grace and kept under
control. From such a style, Wayne's viewers infer reserve, ease,
and self-confidence—and they've come to see these qualities as
being the real John Wayne, not an actor's performance.

Equally important, John Wayne's roles and the stories in which
he appeared create a consistent hero for film viewers. If his
physical presence communicates certain human qualities, his
films present patterns of storytelling about similar types of
characters which augment those qualities. From these repeated
narrative patterns, other meanings and values accrue to Wayne's
image. Most of his B and A films tell one basic story in a handful
of variations. This basic "John Wayne" story tells of an outsider
who is able to overcome a dark past or personal flaw to join a
family or a community, often even to save that group. Typically,
Wayne's hero is outside the community because he is an outlaw,
because he is running away from failure, because he is an isolated
leader, because he is stubborn and difficult, or because he is
aging. Wayne himself comments on the development of this type:

> Let me explain something that happened in my career.
> They've never made a point of this, but I have tried never
> to play the pure hero. I have always been a character of some
> kind. When I started doing these quickie Westerns . . . listen,
> Tom Mix and Buck Jones and Tim McCoy put their white
> hat on and their gloves, and they stood and waited for the
> fella to get up and he could hit them with a chair and everything
> else, and they were just clean and pure. Well, my dad told
> me if I got in a fight to win the goddamn thing. When I went
> into Westerns I didn't like to wear the rodeo clothes, so I started

wearing levis. . . . But these are the things I did in my way that never really came out in public.

What I was starting to say was that was antihero, what I just told you about busting chairs over guys and not wearing fancy clothes which kind of dropped the character down. In every picture that I've done I've tried to have some human weaknesses and admit those human weaknesses.[18]

In most variations of his story, the Wayne character is able to overcome his weaknesses only for the moment, to save others and restore community. Then this loner is destined to move on (or die), to remain an outsider, because his kind of man cannot function in a civilized world. Critic Andrew Sarris analyzes the appeal of such a hero:

I remember responding to him in a relatively uncomplicated way though he seldom functioned as a conventional hero. He could be accursed or obsessed. . . . And on many other occasions the characters he played faced a twilight existence of loneliness and dependency. . . . Wayne's most enduring image, however, is that of the displaced loner vaguely uncomfortable with the very civilization he is helping to establish and preserve. . . . At his first appearance we usually sense a very private person with some wound, loss, or grievance from the past.[19]

Many of Wayne's films after the late 1940's incorporate an important variation of this hero, one whose weaknesses are linked to aging. Beginning with *Red River* (1948), the majority of his roles depict Wayne as an older character in one of three patterns: He plays a man roughly his own age who is the oldest in a group, and hence the leader-father figure. He plays an older man whose most important human relationships and heroics are in the past. Or he plays a man who comes to old age in a period he no longer suits, the Wayne hero as anachronism. Particularly by the 1960's, his characters embodied self-conscious commentary on the aging

Wayne hero as part of the past. Sometimes this comment is ironic, as in *True Grit*, where Wayne's "fat old man" can still outfight and outwit younger adversaries. Sometimes it is elegiac, as in *The Shootist*, where his gunfighter lives by a personal code which will die with him. Through such stories, Wayne's hero came to signify not only the outsider in society, but also an outsider in time, belonging only to the past—usually the past of a romanticized nineteenth-century American West. As Terry Curtis Fox puts it,

> With age . . . the very qualities that made Wayne a star in the first place and a political symbol in the second—his intransigence, his moral authority, his ability to suggest an inordinate sorrow beneath a heroic exterior—would serve to identify Wayne with a mythical America of moral certainty and individual power. The older Wayne got, the more he could embody the American past.[20]

In general, the plots of his films focus on a heroic man of admirable individual strength and character who nevertheless does not achieve a full life with a happy ending. Thus, often the typical Wayne story seems not to affirm the rugged individualism Wayne's hero embodies, yet the *importance* of such a hero to the group *is* affirmed, and the plots present this hero as admirable through Wayne's commanding presence and his central place in the resolution of the story. John Wayne, the real man and the actor, became so blended with this hero, that he, too, took on heroic importance to *his* society—contemporary American society. He, too, assumed value as someone different from most in his uncompromising standards, bravery, and strength.

The retelling of a story about a similar character creates a myth, and the movie-going public of the forties, fifties, and sixties knew the mythic Wayne that emerged from the scores of films he made in these decades. Coupled with the power of his physical presence, the power of this mythic figure set a "John Wayne" in the public mind that would never be dislodged, only enlarged. John Wayne became essentially the same person as "John Wayne."

Studio publicity and eventually Wayne himself asserted the identity of the myth and the real person.

If Wayne had been a reclusive star, able or inclined to avoid publicity, the myth articulated by his physical presence and typical roles would be the image which American culture enjoyed, knowing it to be a fiction. Of course, such was not the case. As an actor who began his career during the studio era of Hollywood, he gained an image largely produced by studio executives and publicity agents. For example, fan magazine articles publicizing his first starring role in the 1931 film, *The Big Trail*, credit his "striking appearance"[21] and his "height and his rangy build, his manly, open countenance"[22] with attracting the role. One describes how he went through his screen tests "with a great deal of courage and patience."[23] Wayne is quoted, saying the same sort of thing about his acting that would be the "truth" for decades: "I knew there was no use trying to act . . . because I didn't know a thing about it. But I figured that if they liked me as I am—just being natural—I'd get along all right."[24] In short, Wayne's physical presence, his strong character, and his natural performing abilities form his image from the start. And the correspondence between the real and screen Wayne emerges then, too: "John is just as he looks. Simple and forthright, appreciative and loyal—a good boy, with all the steadfastness that could be expected of a young pioneer, and much more humor."[25] Over the next decades, publicity and fan magazine coverage offer the same manly, attractive image, adding stories of personal difficulties to be overcome, first as husband and father and then as aging, ill star.

When he became an independent star and producer, he sustained this invented self. He added his political beliefs, by being outspoken and by making films rooted in their values. By then, the distinction between a private, or "real," Wayne and the mythic, or "movie," Wayne had been permanently blurred. Wayne maintained and lived out that blurring between the personal and a movie reality. Thus, on and off the screen, he was known as an aggressive individualist in both profession and politics, as a family man struggling with the difficulties of holding together that family, as an aging hero in illness and death, and as an emblem of vanishing American values. One small, but telling, illustration can be read in his son Michael's explanation of why Wayne hadn't won an Oscar for many years:

> He wasn't really a part of Hollywood in the strictest sense. He wasn't a part of the Bel Air circuit; he was an individual. He didn't live in Los Angeles; he lived in Newport Beach and for a long time he wasn't even a member of the Motion Picture Academy. So he wasn't a really fair-haired boy. He was quite outspoken and he had a completely different political point of view from most of the people in town.[26]

Of course, the elements of this image of Wayne—one even his son gives credence to—parallel the attributes of the movie hero discussed above: the strong loner who can't fit in family or community, but who provides an exemplary ideal for others, mythic in stature. That hero stepped off the screen to attain a larger reality in American culture. British writer Barry Norman characterizes Wayne's appeal:

> What happens is that a movie star creates an illusion; the audience believes it and eventually the star can come to believe what the audience believes. And that, I think, is what happened with John Wayne. . . .
> Wayne's shadow, cast huge on the screen, looked like the epitome of the all-American male and so the legend arose that the substance was the same. That's why they have put up all those statues—not to the man, not to the actor, but to a legend.
> John Wayne would surely have approved; because in the end I think he, too, came to believe the legend.[27]

Of course, what Wayne believed in the end can't be known with certainty. In his last interview, given to Barbara Walters, he responds in ambiguous ways to her questions about his real and screen selves. She asks him whether ". . . the guy we see on screen, is he now you?" He answers, "Yeah, I think so."[28] But she also asks how he feels when ". . . people call you the legend, or the legendary John Wayne . . . I mean do you feel as if they're writing about a monument, or a man who isn't there anymore?" To this, he responds in less certain words to separate himself from his image: "Well, yeah, that is kind of scary. . . . They talk like you're a part of the past or something. And rightfully so; I am a part of the past. But I also want to be a little part of the future, too."[29]

Clearly, by the end of his life and career, John Wayne had come to mean more to the American public than can be explained by the movies he made. The cumulative meaning of his performances, his roles, and his real-life behavior created an image that could carry mythic values in the society. Different elements of society respond to the myth in different ways, but they see Wayne *as* that myth whether they value it or not. And even if one person may dislike Wayne's conservative politics or Hollywood star acting persona, while another cherishes them, all seem to value the perceived integrity of the "real" person himself.

## NOTES

1. Maurice Zolotow, *Shooting Star: A Biography of John Wayne* (New York: Simon and Schuster, 1974; rev. ed. 1979) 427.

2. Donald Shepherd and Robert Slatzer, *Duke: The Life and Times of John Wayne* (Garden City, New York: Doubleday, 1985) 285.

3. John Belton, "John Wayne: As Sure as the Turning o' the Earth," *Velvet Light Trap*, 7 (Winter 72-73): 26.

4. Thomas B. Morgan, "God and Man in Hollywood," in *Self-Creations: Thirteen Impersonalities* (New York: Holt, Rinehart, and Winston, 1965) 207.

5. "John Wayne: Everybody's Hero," *The Saturday Evening Post*, September 1979: 37.

6. Terry Curtis Fox, "People We Like: The Duke of Deception," *Film Comment*, 15 (Sept-Oct 1979): 68.

7. Joan Didion, "John Wayne: A Love Song," *The Saturday Evening Post*, 14 August 1965: 76.

8. Kingsley Canham, *The Hollywood Professionals: Michael Curtiz, Raoul Walsh, Henry Hathaway* (New York: A. S. Barnes, 1973) 173.

9. John Boswell and Jay David, *Duke: The John Wayne Album* (New York: Ballantine, 1979) 75.

10. Boswell and David 75.

11. F. Anthony Macklin, " 'I Come Ready': An Interview with John Wayne," *Film Heritage*, 19 (Summer 1975): 17.

12. Zolotow 248.

13. Allen Eyles, *John Wayne* (New York: A. S. Barnes, 1976; rev. ed. 1979) 12.

14. Andrew Sarris, "John Wayne's Strange Legacy: A Revisionist View," *The New Republic*, 4 August 1979: 34.

15. Barbara Walters, "The Barbara Walters Show," ABC, 13 March 1979, interview transcript quoted in Pat Stacy, *Duke: A Love Story* (New York: Atheneum, 1983) 153.

16. Fox 68. See Richard Dyer, *Stars* (London: BFI, 1979) 165–167, for an interesting semiotic analysis of Wayne's performance "signs."

17. Sarris 34.

18. Macklin 14, 15.

19. Sarris 34.

20. Fox 70.

21. Harry N. Blair, "Three Boys Who Won," *The New Movie Magazine*, February 1931: 51.

22. Elisabeth Goldbeck, "Samson of Hollywood: John Wayne Needed a Haircut and Became Famous," *Motion Picture*, February 1931: 76.

23. Goldbeck 112.

24. Goldbeck 76.

25. Goldbeck 112.

26. Barry Norman, "John Wayne: An American Legend," *The Film Greats* (London: Hodder and Stoughton, BBC, 1985) 147–148.

27. Norman 153.

28. Quoted in Stacy 153.

29. Quoted in Stacy 152.

# 3

# INTERVIEW: AN "AMERICAN" VOICE

This interview, published in May 1971, was mildly infamous at the time. Wayne had to defend the implied racism and hard-nosed politics of his statements to readers and subsequent interviewers. In spite of its reputation, the interview is a good one. Although the heat of Vietnam politics has cooled and some of Wayne's film stories are fuzzy,[1] it remains his most intriguing public statement. The *Playboy* editors (with the aid of good tequila, it seems) provoke a pugnacious Wayne. The actor's voice is rough and more self-revealing than in other interviews; his comments also show Wayne's awareness of his role in American culture. Other interviewers, in awe or intimidated, have drawn from him more details of film making, but none has elicited quite the full sense of the Wayne personality expressed here.[2]

## *PLAYBOY* INTERVIEW: JOHN WAYNE

### a candid conversation with the straight-shooting superstar/superpatriot

For more than 41 years, the barrel-chested physique and laconic derring-do of John Wayne have been prototypical of gung-ho virility, Hollywood style. In more than 200 films—from *The Big Trail* in 1930 to the soon-to-be-released *Million Dollar Kidnapping*³—Wayne has charged the beaches at Iwo Jima, beaten back the Indians at Fort Apache and bloodied his fists in the name of frontier justice so often—and with nary a defeat—that he has come to occupy a unique niche in American folklore. The older generation still remembers him as Singing Sandy, one of the screen's first crooning cowpokes; the McLuhan generation has grown up with him on "The Late Show." With Cooper and Gable and Tracy gone, the last of the legendary stars survives and flourishes as never before.

His milieu is still the action Western, in which Wayne's simplistic plotlines and easily discernible good and bad guys attest to a romantic way of life long gone from the American scene—if indeed it ever really existed. Even his screen name—changed from Marion Michael Morrison—conveys the man's plain, rugged cinematic personality. Fittingly, he was the first of the Western movie heroes to poke a villain in the jaw. Wearing the symbolic white Stetson—which never seemed to fall off, even in the wildest combat—he made scores of three-and-a-half day formula oaters such as *Pals of the Saddle* in the Thirties before being tapped by director John Ford to star in *Stagecoach*—the 1939 classic that paved the way for his subsequent success in such milestone Westerns as *Red River*, the ultimate epic of the cattle drive, and *The Alamo*, a patriotic paean financed by Wayne with $1,500,000 of his own money.

By 1969, having made the list of Top Ten box-office attractions for 19 consecutive years, Wayne had grossed more than $400,000,000 for his studios—more than any other star in motion-picture history. But because of his uncompromising squareness—and his archconservative politics—he was still largely a profit without honor in Hollywood. That oversight was belatedly rectified when his peers voted the tearful star a 1970 Oscar for his portrayal of Rooster Cogburn, the tobacco-chewing, hard-drinking, straight-shooting, patch-eyed marshal in *True Grit*—a possibly unwitting exercise in self-parody that good-naturedly spoofed dozens of his past characterizations. President Nixon remarked several months later at a press conference that he and his family had recently enjoyed a screening of *Chisum*, adding: "I think that John Wayne is a very fine actor."

Long active in Republican politics, Wayne has vigorously campaigned and helped raise funds for Nixon, Ronald Reagan, George Murphy, Barry Goldwater and Los Angeles' maverick Democratic mayor Sam Yorty. Before the 1968 campaign, a right-wing Texas billionaire had urged Wayne to serve as Vice-Presidential running mate to George Wallace, an overture he rejected. Not least among the Texan's reasons for wanting to draft Wayne was the actor's obdurately hawkish support of the Indochina war—as glorified in his production of *The Green Berets*, which had the dubious distinction of being probably the only pro-war movie made in Hollywood during the Sixties.

Last fall, Wayne's first television special—a 90-minute quasi-historical pageant dripping with God-home-and-country hyperbole—racked up such a hefty Nielsen rating that it was rebroadcast in April. At year's end, Wayne was named one of the nation's most admired entertainers in a Gallup Poll. Assigned by *PLAYBOY* shortly afterward to interview the superstar, Contributing Editor Richard Warren Lewis journeyed to Wayne's sprawling (11-room, seven-bath) $175,000 bayfront residence on the Gold Coast of Newport Beach, California, where he lives with his third Latin wife—Peruvian-born Pilar Pallete [*sic*–Palette]—and three of his seven children. Of his subject Lewis writes:

"Wayne greeted me on a manicured lawn against a backdrop of sailboats, motor cruisers and yachts plying Newport harbor. Wearing a realistic toupee, Wayne at first appeared considerably younger than he is; only the liver spots on both hands and the lines in his jut-jawed face told of his 63 years. But at six feet, four and 244 pounds, it still almost seems as if he *could* have single-handedly mopped up all those bad guys from the Panhandle to Guadalcanal. His sky-blue eyes, though somewhat rheumy from the previous night's late hours, reinforced the image.

"Adjourning to the breakfast room, we spoke for several hours while Wayne enjoyed the first Dungeness crabs of the season, drank black coffee and fielded phone calls. One of the calls settled details of an imminent visit from the Congolese ambassador. (Wayne and several associates own lucrative mineral rights in the Congo.) Another call confirmed a $100 bet on the Santa Anita Handicap, to be contested later that day. (Wayne lost.)

" 'Christ, we better get going,' he said shortly before one o'clock. 'They're holding lunch for us.' He led the way past a den and trophy room stacked with such memorabilia as photos of his 18 grandchildren and the largest collection of Hopi Indian *katcina* dolls west of Barry Goldwater. Outside the house, past jacaranda and palm trees and a kidney-shaped swimming pool, we reached a seven-foot-high concrete wall at the entryway and boarded Wayne's darkgreen Bonneville station wagon, a production model with only two modifications—a sun roof raised six inches to accommodate the driver's ten-gallon hat, and two telephone channels at the console beside him.

"At Newport harbor, we boarded Wayne's awesome Wild Goose II, a converted U.S. Navy mine sweeper that saw service during the last six months of World War Two and has been refitted as a pleasure cruiser. After a quick tour of the 136-foot vessel— which included a look at the twin 500-horsepower engines, clattering teletype machines (A.P., U.P.I., Reuter's, Tass) on the bridge disgorging wire dispatches, and the lavishly appointed bedroom and dressing suites—we were seated at a polished-walnut table in the main saloon.

"Over a high-protein diet lunch of char-broiled steak, lettuce and cottage cheese, Wayne reminisced about the early days of Hollywood, when he was making two-reelers for $500 each. Later that afternoon, he produced a bottle of his favorite tequila. One of the eight crew members anointed our glasses with a dash of fresh lemon juice, coarse salt and heaping ice shards that, Wayne said, had been chopped from a 1000-year-old glacier on a recent Wild Goose visit to Alaska. Sustained by these potent drinks, our conversation—ranging from Wayne's early days in film making

to the current state of the industry—continued until dusk, and
resumed a week later in the offices of Wayne's Batjac Productions,
on the grounds of Paramount Pictures—one of the last of
Hollywood's rapidly dwindling contingent of major studios."

*PLAYBOY*: How do you feel about the state of the motion-picture business today?

*WAYNE*: I'm glad I won't be around much longer to see what
they do with it. The men who control the big studios today are
stock manipulators and bankers. They know nothing about our
business. They're in it for the buck. The only thing they can do
is say, "Jeez, that picture with what's-her-name running around
the park naked made money, so let's make another one. If that's
what they want, let's give it to them." Some of these guys remind
me of highclass whores. Look at 20th Century-Fox, where they're
making movies like *Myra Breckinridge*. Why doesn't that son of
a bitch Darryl Zanuck get himself a striped silk shirt and learn
how to play the piano? Then he could work in any room in the
house. As much as I couldn't stand some of the old-time moguls—
especially Harry Cohn—these men took an interest in the future
of their business. They had integrity. There was a stretch when
they realized that they'd made a hero out of the goddamn gangster
heavy in crime movies, that they were doing a discredit to our
country. So the moguls voluntarily took it upon themselves to stop
making gangster movies. No censorship from the outside. They
were responsible to the public. But today's executives don't give
a damn. In their efforts to grab the box office that these sex
pictures are attracting, they're producing garbage. They're taking
advantage of the fact that nobody wants to be called a bluenose.
But they're going to reach the point where the American people
will say, "The hell with this!" And once they do, we'll have
censorship in every state, in every city, and there'll be no way
you can make a worthwhile picture for adults and have it
acceptable for national release.

*PLAYBOY*: Won't the present rating system prevent that from happening?

*WAYNE*: No. Every time they rate a picture, they let a little more go. Ratings are ridiculous to begin with. There was no need for rated pictures when the major studios were in control. Movies were once made for the whole family. Now, with the kind of junk the studios are cranking out—and the jacked-up prices they're charging for the privilege of seeing it—the average family is staying home and watching television. I'm quite sure that within two or three years, Americans will be completely fed up with these perverted films.

*PLAYBOY*: What kind of films do you consider perverted?

*WAYNE*: Oh, *Easy Rider*, *Midnight Cowboy*—that kind of thing. Wouldn't you say that the wonderful love of those two men in *Midnight Cowboy*, a story about two fags, qualifies? But don't get me wrong. As far as a man and a woman is concerned, I'm awfully happy there's a thing called sex. It's an extra something God gave us. I see no reason why it shouldn't be in pictures. Healthy, lusty sex is wonderful.

*PLAYBOY*: How graphically do you think it should be depicted on the screen?

*WAYNE*: When you get hairy, sweaty bodies in the foreground, it becomes distasteful, unless you use a pretty heavy gauze. I can remember seeing pictures that Ernst Lubitsch made in the Thirties that were beautifully risqué—and you'd certainly send your children to see them. They were done with *intimation*. They got over everything these other pictures do without showing the hair and the sweat. When you think of the wonderful picture fare we've had through the years and realize we've come to this shit, it's disgusting. If they want to continue making those pictures, fine. But my career will have ended. I've already reached a pretty good height right now in a business that I feel is going to fade out from its own vulgarity.

*PLAYBOY*: Don't gory films like *The Wild Bunch* also contribute to that vulgarity?

*WAYNE*: Certainly. To me, *The Wild Bunch* was distasteful. It would have been a good picture without the gore. Pictures go too far when they use that kind of realism, when they have shots of blood spurting out and teeth flying, and when they throw liver out to make it look like people's insides. *The Wild Bunch* was one of the first to go that far in realism, and the curious went to see it. That may make the bankers and the stock promoters think this is a necessary ingredient for successful motion pictures. They seem to forget the one basic principle of our business—illusion. We're in the business of magic. I don't think it hurts a child to see anything that has the *illusion* of violence in it. All our fairy tales have some kind of violence—the good knight riding to kill the dragon, etc. Why do we have to show the knight spreading the serpent's guts all over the candy mountain?

*PLAYBOY*: Proponents of screen realism say that a public inured to bloody war-news footage on television isn't going to accept the mere illusion of violence in movies.

*WAYNE*: Perhaps we *have* run out of imagination on how to effect illusion because of the satiating realism of a real war on television. But haven't we got *enough* of that in real life? Why can't the same point be made just as effectively in a drama without all the gore? The violence in my pictures, for example, is lusty and a little bit humorous, because I believe humor nullifies violence. Like in one picture, directed by Henry Hathaway, this heavy was sticking a guy's head in a barrel of water. I'm watching this and I don't like it one bit, so I pick up this pick handle and I yell, "Hey!" and cock him across the head. Down he went—with no spurting blood. Well, that got a hell of a laugh because of the way I did it. That's my kind of violence.

*PLAYBOY*: Audiences may like your kind of violence on the screen, but they'd never heard profanity in a John Wayne movie until *True Grit*. Why did you finally decide to use such earthy language in a film?

*WAYNE*: In my other pictures, we've had an explosion or something go off when a bad word was said. This time we didn't. It's profanity, all right, but I doubt if there's anybody in the United States who hasn't heard the expression son of a bitch or bastard. We felt it was acceptable in this instance. At the emotional high point in that particular picture, I felt it was OK to use it. It would have been pretty hard to say "you illegitimate sons of so-and-so!"

*PLAYBOY*: In the past, you've often said that if the critics liked one of your films, you must be doing something wrong. But *True Grit* was almost unanimously praised by the critics. Were you doing something wrong? Or were they right for a change?

*WAYNE*: Well, I knew that *True Grit* was going to go—even with the critics. Once in a while, you come onto a story that has such great humor. The author caught the flavor of Mark Twain, to my way of thinking.

*PLAYBOY*: The reviewers thought you set out to poke fun at your own image in *True Grit*.

*WAYNE*: It wasn't really a parody. Rooster Cogburn's attitude toward life was maybe a little different, but he was basically the same character I've always played.

*PLAYBOY*: Do you think *True Grit* is the best film you've ever made?

*WAYNE*: No, I don't. Two classic Westerns were better—*Stagecoach* and *Red River*—and a third, *The Searchers*, which I thought deserved more praise than it got, and *The Quiet Man* was certainly one of the best. Also the one that all the college cinematography students run all the time—*The Long Voyage Home*.

*PLAYBOY*: Which was the worst?

*WAYNE*: Well, there's about 50 of them that are tied. I can't even remember the names of some of the leading ladies in those first ones, let alone the names of the pictures.

*PLAYBOY*: At what point in your career were you nicknamed Duke?

*WAYNE*: That goes back to my childhood. I was called Duke after a dog—a very good Airedale out of the Baldwin Kennels. Republic Pictures gave me a screen credit on one of the early pictures and called me Michael Burn. On another one, they called me Duke Morrison. Then they decided Duke Morrison didn't have enough prestige. My real name, Marion Michael Morrison, didn't sound American enough for them. So they came up with John Wayne. I didn't have any say in it, but I think it's a great name. It's short and strong and to the point. It took me a long time to get used to it, though. I still don't recognize it when somebody calls me John.

*PLAYBOY*: After giving you a new name, did the studio decide on any particular screen image for you?

*WAYNE*: They made me a singing cowboy. The fact that I couldn't sing—or play the guitar—became terribly embarrassing to me, especially on personal appearances. Every time I made a public appearance, the kids insisted that I sing *The Desert Song* or something. But I couldn't take along the fella who played the guitar out one side of the camera and the fella who sang on the other side of the camera. So finally I went to the head of the studio and said, "Screw this, I can't handle it." And I quit doing those kind of pictures. They went out and brought the best hillbilly recording artist in the country to Hollywood to take my place. For the first couple of pictures, they had a hard time selling him, but he finally caught on. His name was Gene Autry. It was 1939 before I made *Stagecoach*—the picture that really made me a star.

*PLAYBOY*: Like *Stagecoach*, most of the 204⁴ pictures you've made—including your latest, *Rio Lobo*—have been Westerns. Don't the plots all start to seem the same?

*WAYNE*: *Rio Lobo* certainly wasn't any different from most of my Westerns. Nor was *Chisum*, the one before that. But there still seems to be a very hearty public appetite for this kind of film—what some writers call a typical John Wayne Western. That's a label they use disparagingly.

*PLAYBOY*: Does that bother you?

*WAYNE*: Nope. If I depended on the critics' judgment and recognition, I'd never have gone into the motion-picture business.

*PLAYBOY*: Did last year's Academy Award for *True Grit* mean a lot to you?

*WAYNE*: Sure it did—even if it took the industry 40 years to get around to it. But I think both of my two previous Oscar nominations—for *She Wore a Yellow Ribbon* and *Sands of Iwo Jima*—were worthy of the honor. I know the Marines and all the American Armed Forces were quite proud of my portrayal of Stryker, the Marine sergeant in *Iwo*. At an American Legion convention in Florida, General MacArthur told me, "You represent the American Serviceman better than the American Serviceman himself." And, at 42, in *She Wore a Yellow Ribbon*, I played the same character that I played in *True Grit* at 62. But I really didn't need an Oscar. I'm a box-office champion with a record they're going to have to run to catch. And they won't.

*PLAYBOY*: A number of critics claim that your record rests on your appeal to adolescents. Do you think that's true?

*WAYNE*: Let's say I hope that I appeal to the more carefree times in a person's life rather than to his reasoning adulthood. I'd just like to be an image that reminds someone of joy rather than of the problems of the world.

*PLAYBOY*: Do you think young people still feel strongly about you?

*WAYNE*: Luckily, so far, it seems they kind of consider me an older friend, somebody believable and down-to-earth. I've avoided being mean or petty, but I've never avoided being rough or tough. I've only played one cautious part in my life, in *Allegheny Uprising*. My parts have ranged from that rather dull character to Ralls in *Wake of the Red Witch*, who was a nice enough fella sober, but bestial when he was drunk, and certainly a rebel. I was also a rebel in *Reap the Wild Wind* with De Mille. I've played many parts in which I've rebelled against something in society. I was never much of a joiner. Kids do join things, but they also like to consider themselves capable of thinking for themselves. So do I.

*PLAYBOY*: But isn't your kind of screen rebellion very different from that of today's young people?

*WAYNE*: Sure. Mine is personal rebellion against the monotony of life, against the status quo. The rebellion in these kids—especially in the SDSers and those groups—seems to be a kind of dissension by rote.

*PLAYBOY*: Meaning what?

*WAYNE*: Just this: The articulate liberal group has caused certain things in our country, and I wonder how long the young people who read *PLAYBOY* are going to allow these things to go on. George Putnam, the Los Angeles news analyst, put it quite succinctly when he said, "What kind of a nation is it that fails to understand that freedom of speech and assembly are one thing, and anarchy and treason are quite another, that allows known Communists to serve as teachers to pervert the natural loyalties and ideals of our kids, filling them with fear and doubt and hate and downgrading patriotism and all our heroes of the past?"

*PLAYBOY*: You blame all this on liberals?

*WAYNE*: Well, the liberals seem to be quite willing to have Communists teach their kids in school. The Communists realized that they couldn't start a workers' revolution in the United States, since the workers were too affluent and too progressive. So the Commies decided on the next-best thing, and that's to start on the schools, start on the kids. And they've managed to do it. They're already in colleges; now they're getting into high schools. I wouldn't mind if they taught my children the basic philosophy of communism, in theory and how it works in actuality. But I don't want somebody like Angela Davis inculcating an enemy doctrine in my kids' minds.

*PLAYBOY*: Angela Davis claims that those who would revoke her teaching credentials on ideological grounds are actually discriminating against her because she's black. Do you think there's any truth in that?

WAYNE: With a lot of blacks, there's quite a bit of resentment along with their dissent, and possibly rightfully so. But we can't all of a sudden get down on our knees and turn everything over to the leadership of the blacks. I believe in white supremacy until the blacks are educated to a point of responsibility. I don't believe in giving authority and positions of leadership and judgment to irresponsible people.

PLAYBOY: Are you equipped to judge which blacks are irresponsible and which of their leaders inexperienced?

WAYNE: It's not my judgment. The academic community has developed certain tests that determine whether the blacks are sufficiently equipped scholastically. But some blacks have tried to force the issue and enter college when they haven't passed the tests and don't have the requisite background.

PLAYBOY: How do they get that background?

WAYNE: By going to school. I don't know why people insist that blacks have been forbidden their right to go to school. They were allowed in public schools wherever I've been. Even if they don't have the proper credentials for college, there are courses to help them become eligible. But if they aren't academically ready for that step, I don't think they should be allowed in. Otherwise, the academic society is brought down to the lowest common denominator.

PLAYBOY: But isn't it true that we're never likely to rectify the inequities in our educational system until some sort of remedial education is given to disadvantaged minority groups?

WAYNE: What good would it do to register anybody in a class of higher algebra or calculus if they haven't learned to count? There has to be a standard. I don't feel guilty about the fact that five or ten generations ago these people were slaves. Now, I'm not condoning slavery. It's just a fact of life, like the kid who gets infantile paralysis and has to wear braces, so he can't play football with the rest of us. I will say this, though I think any black who can compete with a white today can get a better break than a white man. I wish they'd tell me where in the world they have it better than right here in America.

*PLAYBOY*: Many militant blacks would argue that they have it better almost *anywhere* else. Even in Hollywood, they feel that the color barrier is still up for many kinds of jobs. Do you limit the number of blacks you use in your pictures?

*WAYNE*: Oh, Christ no. I've directed two pictures and I gave the blacks their proper position. I had a black slave in *The Alamo*, and I had a correct number of blacks in *The Green Berets*. If it's supposed to be a black character, naturally I use a black actor. But I don't go so far as hunting for positions for them. I think the Hollywood studios are carrying their tokenism a little too far. There's no doubt that ten percent of the population is black, or colored, or whatever they want to call themselves; they certainly aren't Caucasian. Anyway, I suppose there should be the same percentage of the colored race in films as in society. But it can't always be that way. There isn't necessarily going to be ten percent of the grips or sound men who are black, because more than likely, ten percent haven't trained themselves for that type of work.

*PLAYBOY*: Can blacks be integrated into the film industry if they are denied training and education?

*WAYNE*: It's just as hard for a white man to get a card in the Hollywood craft unions.

*PLAYBOY*: That's hardly the point, but let's change the subject. For years American Indians have played an important—if subordinate—role in your Westerns. Do you feel any empathy with them?

*WAYNE*: I don't feel we did wrong in taking this great country away from them, if that's what you're asking. Our so-called stealing of this country from them was just a matter of survival.

There were great numbers of people who needed new land, and the Indians were selfishly trying to keep it for themselves.

*PLAYBOY*: Weren't the Indians—by virtue of prior possession—the rightful owners of the land?

*WAYNE*: Look, I'm sure there have been inequalities. If those inequalities are presently affecting any of the Indians now alive, they have a right to a court hearing. But what happened 100 years ago in our country can't be blamed on us today.

*PLAYBOY*: Indians today are still being dehumanized on reservations.

*WAYNE*: I'm quite sure that the concept of a Government-run reservation would have an ill effect on anyone. But that seems to be what the socialists are working for now—to have *everyone* cared for from cradle to grave.

*PLAYBOY*: Indians on reservations are more neglected than cared for. Even if you accept the principle of expropriation, don't you think a more humane solution to the Indian problem could have been devised?

*WAYNE*: This may come as a surprise to you, but I wasn't alive when reservations were created—even if I *do* look that old. I have no idea what the best method of dealing with the Indians in the 1800's would have been. Our forefathers evidently thought they were doing the right thing.

*PLAYBOY*: Do you think the Indians encamped on Alcatraz have a right to that land?

*WAYNE*: Well, I don't know of anybody else who wants it. The fellas who were taken off it sure don't want to go back there, including the guards. So as far as I'm concerned, I think we ought to make a deal with the Indians. They should pay as much for Alcatraz as we paid them for Manhattan. I hope they haven't been careless with their wampum.

*PLAYBOY*: How do you feel about the Government grant for a university and cultural center that these Indians have demanded as "reparations"?

*WAYNE*: What happened between their forefathers and our forefathers is so far back—right, wrong or indifferent—that I don't see why we owe them anything. I don't know why the Government should give them something that it wouldn't give me.

*PLAYBOY*: Do you think they've had the same advantages and opportunities that you've had?

*WAYNE*: I'm not gonna give you one of those I-was-a-poor-boy-and-I-pulled-myself-up-by-my-bootstraps stories, but I've gone without a meal or two in my life, and I still don't expect the Government to turn over any of its territory to me. Hard times aren't something I can blame my fellow citizens for. Years ago, I didn't have all the opportunities, either. But you can't whine and bellyache 'cause somebody else got a good break and you didn't, like these Indians are. We'll *all* be on a reservation soon if the socialists keep subsidizing groups like them with our tax money.

*PLAYBOY*: In your distaste for socialism, aren't you overlooking the fact that many worthwhile and necessary Government services—such as Social Security and Medicare—derived from essentially socialistic programs evolved during the Thirties?

*WAYNE*: I know all about that. In the late Twenties, when I was a sophomore at USC, I was a socialist myself—but not when I left. The average college kid idealistically wishes everybody could have ice cream and cake for every meal. But as he gets older and gives more thought to his and his fellow man's responsibilities, he finds that it can't work out that way—that some people just won't carry their load.

*PLAYBOY*: What about welfare recipients?

*WAYNE*: I believe in welfare—a welfare *work* program. I don't think a fella should be able to sit on his backside and receive welfare. I'd like to know why well-educated idiots keep apologizing for lazy and complaining people who think the world owes them a living. I'd like to know why they make excuses for cowards who spit in the faces of the police and then run behind the judicial sob sisters. I can't understand these people who carry placards to save the life of some criminal, yet have no thought for the innocent victim.

*PLAYBOY*: Who are "these people" you're talking about?

*WAYNE*: Entertainers like Steve Allen and his cronies who went up to Northern California and held placards to save the life of that guy Caryl Chessman. I just don't understand these things. I can't understand why our national leadership isn't willing to take the responsibility of leadership instead of checking polls and listening to the few that scream. Why are we allowing ourselves to become a mobocracy instead of a democracy? When you allow unlawful acts to go unpunished, you're moving toward a government of men rather than a government of law; you're moving toward anarchy. And that's exactly what we're doing. We allow dirty loudmouths to publicly call policemen pigs; we let a fella like William Kunstler make a speech to the Black Panthers saying that the ghetto is theirs, and that if police come into it, they have a right to shoot them. Why is that dirty, no-good son of a bitch allowed to practice law?

*PLAYBOY*: What's your source for that statement you attribute to Kunstler?

*WAYNE*: It appeared in a Christian Anti-Communism Crusade letter written by Fred Schwarz on August 1, 1969. Here, I'll read it to you: "The notorious leftwing attorney, Bill Kunstler, spoke on political prisoners and political freedom at the National Conference for a United Front Against Fascism, which was held in Oakland, California, July 18, 19 and 20, 1969. He urged blacks to kill white policemen when they entered the black ghetto. He told the story of how a white policeman, John Gleason, was stomped to death in Plainfield, New Jersey. The crowd broke into prolonged applause. Kunstler proceeded to state that, in his opinion, Gleason deserved that death. . . . Kunstler pointed out that no white policeman has set foot in the black ghetto of Plainfield, New Jersey, since July 1967." That could turn out to be a terrible thing he said. Pretty soon there'll be a bunch of whites who'll say, "Well, if that's their land, then this is ours. They'd better not trespass on it." It can work two ways.

*PLAYBOY*: What's your opinion of the stated goals of the Black Panthers?

*WAYNE*: Quite obviously, they represent a danger to society. They're a violent group of young men and women—adventurous, opinionated and dedicated—and they throw their disdain in our face. Now, I hear some of these liberals saying they'd like to be held as white hostages in the Black Panther offices and stay there so that they could see what happens on the early-morning police raids. It might be a better idea for these good citizens to go *with* the police on a raid. When they search a Panther hideout for firearms, let these do-gooders knock and say, "Open the door in the name of the law" and get shot at.

*PLAYBOY*: Why do you think many young people—black and white—support the Panthers?

*WAYNE*: They're standing up for what they *feel* is right, not for what they *think* is right—'cause they don't think. As a kid, the Panther ideas probably would have intrigued me. When I was a little kid, you could be adventurous like that without hurting anybody. There were periods when you could blow the valve and let off some steam. Like Halloween. You'd talk about it for three months ahead of time, and then that night you'd go out and stick the hose in the lawn, turn it on and start singing *Old Black Joe* or something. And when people came out from their Halloween party, you'd lift the hose and wet them down. And while you were running, the other kids would be stealing the ice cream from the party. All kinds of rebellious actions like that were accepted for that one day. Then you could talk about it for three months afterward. That took care of about six months of the year. There was another day called the Fourth of July, when you could go out and shoot firecrackers and burn down two or three buildings. So there were two days a year. Now those days are gone. You can't have firecrackers, you can't have explosives, you can't have this—don't do this, don't do that. Don't . . . don't . . . don't. A continual *don't* until the kids are ready to do almost anything rebellious. The Government makes the rules, so now the running of our Government is the thing they're rebelling against. For a lot of those kids, that's just being adventurous. They're not deliberately setting out to undermine the foundations of our great country.

*PLAYBOY*: Is that what you think they're doing?

*WAYNE*: They're doing their level worst—without knowing it. How 'bout all the kids that were at the Chicago Democratic Convention? They were conned into doing hysterical things by a bunch of activists.

*PLAYBOY*: What sort of activists?

*WAYNE*: A lot of Communist-activated people. I know communism's a horrible word to some people. They laugh and say, "He'll be finding them under his bed tomorrow." But perhaps that's because their kid hasn't been inculcated yet. Dr. Herbert Marcuse, the political philosopher at the University of California at San Diego, who is quite obviously a Marxist, put it very succinctly when he said, "We will use the anarchists."

*PLAYBOY*: Why do you think leftist ideologues such as Marcuse have become heroes on so many of the nation's campuses?

*WAYNE*: Marcuse has become a hero only for an articulate clique. The men that give me faith in my country are fellas like Spiro Agnew, not the Marcuses. They've attempted in every way to humiliate Agnew. They've tried the old Rooseveltian thing of trying to laugh him out of political value to his party. Every comedian's taken a crack at him. But I bet if you took a poll today, he'd probably be one of the most popular men in the United States. Nobody likes Spiro Agnew but the people. Yet he and other responsible Government leaders are booed and pelted when they speak on college campuses.

*PLAYBOY:* Beyond the anti-Administration demonstrations on campuses, do you think there's any justification for such tactics as student occupation of college administration offices?

*WAYNE:* One or two percent of the kids is involved in things like that. But they get away with it because ten percent of the teaching community is behind them. I see on TV how, when the police are trying to keep the kids in line, like up at the University of California at Berkeley, all of a sudden there's a bunch of martyr-professors trying to egg the police into violent action.

*PLAYBOY:* If you were faced with such a confrontation, how would you handle it?

*WAYNE:* Well, when I sent to USC, if anybody had gone into the president's office and shit in his wastepaper basket and used the dirt to write vulgar words on the wall, not only the football team but the average kid on campus would have gone to work on the guy. There doesn't seem to be respect for authority anymore; these student dissenters act like children who have to have their own way on everything. They're immature and living in a little world all their own. Just like hippie dropouts, they're afraid to face the real competitive world.

*PLAYBOY:* What makes you, at the age of 63, feel qualified to comment on the fears and motivations of the younger generation?

*WAYNE:* I've experienced a lot of the same things that kids today are going through, and I think many of them admire me because I haven't been afraid to say that I drink a little whiskey, that I've done a lot of things wrong in my life, that I'm as imperfect as they all are. Christ, I don't claim to have the answers, but I feel compelled to bring up the fact that under the guise of doing good, these kids are causing a hell of a lot of irreparable damage, and they're starting something they're not gonna be able to finish. Every bit of rampant anarchy has provoked a little more from somebody else. And when they start shooting policemen, the time has come to start knocking them off, as far as I'm concerned.

*PLAYBOY*: What do you mean by "knocking them off"?

*WAYNE*: I'd throw 'em in the can if I could. But if they try to kill you, I'd sure as hell shoot back. I think we should break up those organizations or make 'em illegal. The American public is getting sick and tired of what these young people are doing. But it's really partly the public's own fault for allowing the permissiveness that's been going on for the past 15 or 20 years. By permissiveness, I mean simply following Dr. Spock's system of raising children. But that kind of permissiveness isn't unique to young people. Our entire society has promoted an "anything goes" attitude in every area of life and in every American institution. Look at the completely irresponsible editorship of our country's newspapers. By looking for provocative things to put on their front pages, they're encouraging these kids to act the way they're acting. I wonder even more about the responsibility of the press when I read about events like the so-called My Lai massacre in Vietnam. The press and the communications system jumped way ahead of the trials. At the time, they made accusations that I doubted they could back up; frankly, I hoped they couldn't. Well, it turns out there may have been something to it. But I could show you pictures of what the North Vietnamese and the Viet Cong are doing to our people over there. I was at a place called Dak Song, where the children were all burned to death by the V.C., and that's not an unusual thing. But for some reason, our newspapers have never printed pictures or stories about it. With all the terrible things that are being done throughout the world, it has to be one little incident in the United States Army—and the use of the word massacre—that causes the uproar.

*PLAYBOY*: Don't you deplore what happened in My Lai?

*WAYNE*: Not only do I deplore it, but so does the Army—which conducted an extensive investigation and charged everyone connected with the alleged crime.

*PLAYBOY*: Does the fact that the Viet Cong have systematically engaged in atrocities excuse our forces for resorting to the same thing?

*WAYNE*: No, absolutely not. But if your men go to a supposedly peaceful village and the occupants start shooting at them, they're going to have to shoot back to defend their own lives.

*PLAYBOY*: The reports say our GIs slaughtered unarmed civilians and babies at My Lai; no one was shooting at them.

*WAYNE*: If, after going into the town, they brutally killed these people, that's one thing. If they were getting shot at from that town and then they fired back, that's a completely different situation. But you're bringing up the stuff that's being debated in the trials. What I resent is that even before the trials, this stuff was even less of a proven fact, yet the newspapers printed it anyway.

*PLAYBOY*: Do you think there's a credibility gap between the way the war has been reported and the way it's actually being fought—on both sides?

*WAYNE*: It's obvious to me, because I've been there. And you'll find that the young veterans who come back from Vietnam have a lot to say that the media haven't told us—even about our allies. These young men know what they're talking about, because they own a piece of that war, and you should ask the man who owns one.

*PLAYBOY*: Many of those young men who "own a piece of that war" never wanted to go to Vietnam in the first place. Do you think our Government is justified in sending them off to fight in an undeclared war?

*WAYNE*: Well, I sure don't know why we send them over to fight and then stop the bombing so they can get shot that much more. We could easily stop the enemy from getting guns and ammunition that we know are being sent by Chinese and Soviet Communists. But we won't do anything to stop it because we're afraid of world opinion. Why in hell should we worry about world opinion when we're trying to help out a country that's asked for our aid? Of course, Senator Fulbright says the South Vietnamese government doesn't represent the people—even though it's been duly elected by those people. How can a man be so swayed to the opposite side? If he were finding fault with the *administration* of our help over there, that I could understand. What I can't understand is this "pull out, pull out, pull out" attitude he's taken. And what makes it worse is that a lot of people accept anything he says without thinking, simply because the Fulbright scholarships have established an intellectual aura around him.

*PLAYBOY*: The majority of the American people, according to every poll, agree with Fulbright that we ought to pull out, and many think we never should have intervened in the first place. Many Southeast Asian experts, including Fulbright, believe that if Ho Chi Minh had been allowed to run Vietnam as he saw fit after the Geneva Accords of 1954, he would have established an accommodation with Peking that would have given us perhaps a nominally Communist nation, but essentially a nationalist, independent government.

*WAYNE*: How? By what example in history can people like Fulbright come to such wishful thinking?

*PLAYBOY*: The example of Tito's Yugoslavia comes immediately to mind. In any case, what gives us the right to decide for the Vietnamese what kind of government they should have?

*WAYNE*: I don't want the U.S. to decide what kind of government they have. But I don't want the Communists to decide, either. And if we didn't help the South Vietnamese government, that's just what they'd do.

*PLAYBOY*: Why couldn't a general election, supervised by some neutral power, be held in both the North and the South to determine what kind of government the people of Vietnam desire?

*WAYNE*: That would be no more practical than if France, after coming to help us in the Revolution, suggested having an election to decide what we wanted to do. It would be an exact parallel. The majority of those living in the Colonies didn't want war at that time. If there had been a general election then, we probably wouldn't be here today. As far as Vietnam is concerned, we've made mistakes. I know of no country that's perfect. But I honestly believe that there's as much need for us to help the Vietnamese as there was to help the Jews in Germany. The only difference is that we haven't had any leadership in this war. All the liberal Senators have stuck their noses in this, and it's out of their bailiwick. They've already put far too many barriers in the way of the military. Our lack of leadership has gone so far that now no one man can come in, face the issue and tell people that we ought to be in an all-out war.

PLAYBOY: Why do you favor an all-out war?

WAYNE: I figure if we're going to send even one man to die, we ought to be in an all-out conflict. If you fight, you fight to win. And the domino theory is something to be reckoned with, too, both in Europe and Asia. Look at what happened in Czechoslovakia and what's happened all through the Balkans. At some point we have to stop communism. So we might as well stop it right now in Vietnam.

PLAYBOY: You're aware, of course, that most military experts, including two recent Secretaries of State, concede that it would be an unwinnable war except at a cost too incalculable to contemplate.

WAYNE: I think you're making a misstatement. Their fear is that Russia would go to war with us if we stopped the Vietnamese. Well, I don't think Russia wants war any more than we do.

PLAYBOY: Three Presidents seem to have agreed that it would be unwise to gamble millions of lives on that assumption. Since you find their leadership lacking, who would you have preferred in the highest office.

WAYNE: Barry Goldwater would at least have been decisive. I know for a fact that he's a truthful man. Before the '64 election, he told me that he said to the Texan, "I don't think we ought to make an issue out of Vietnam because we both know that we're going to probably end up having to send a half a million men over there." Johnson said, "Yeah, that's probably true, Barry, but I've got an election to win." So Barry told the truth and Johnson got elected on a "peace" platform—and then began to ease them in, a few thousand at a time. I wish our friend Fulbright would bring out those points.

If Douglas MacArthur were alive, he also would have handled the Vietnam situation with dispatch. He was a proven administrator, certainly a proven leader. And MacArthur understood what Americans were and what Americans stood for. Had he been elected President, something significant would have happened during his Administration. He would have taken a stand for the United States in world affairs, and he would have stood by it, and we would have been respected for it. I also admired the tie salesman, President Truman. He was a wonderful, feisty guy who'll go down in history as quite an individual. It's a cinch he had great guts when he decided to straighten things out in Korea; it's just too bad that the State Department was able to frighten him out of doing a complete job. Seems to me, politics have entered too much into the decisions of our leadership. I can't understand politicians. They're either yellowing out from taking a stand or using outside pressure to improve their position.

*PLAYBOY*: Is that why you've refused to run for public office yourself?

*WAYNE*: Exactly.

*PLAYBOY*: Is that what you told George Wallace when you were asked to be his running mate on the 1968 American Independent ticket?

*WAYNE*: No, I explained that I was working for the other Wallis—Hal Wallis—the producer of *True Grit*, and that I'd been a Nixon man.

*PLAYBOY*: What do you think of Nixon's performance since then?

*WAYNE*: I think Mr. Nixon is proving himself his own man. I knew he would. I knew him and stuck with him when he was a loser, and I'm sticking with him now that he's a winner. A lot of extreme rightists are saying that he isn't doing enough, but I think he's gradually wading in and getting control of the reins of Government.

*PLAYBOY:* What impressed you about him when you first met him?

*WAYNE:* His reasonableness. When he came into office, there was such a hue and cry over Vietnam, for instance, that it didn't seem possible for a man to take a stand that would quiet down the extreme leftists. He came on the air and explained the situation as it was from the beginning, and then he told the American people—in a logical, reasoning way—what he was going to do. and then he began to do it.

*PLAYBOY:* What he began to do, of course, was "Vietnamize" the war and withdraw American troops. How can you approve of these policies and also advocate all-out war?

*WAYNE:* Well, I don't advocate all-out war if it isn't necessary. All I know is that we as a country should be backing up whatever the proposition is that we sent one man to die for.

*PLAYBOY:* If that view is shared by as many Americans as you seem to think, then why was *The Green Berets*—which has been labeled as your personal statement on the Vietnam war—so universally panned?

*WAYNE:* Because the critics don't like my politics, and they were condemning the war, not the picture. I don't mean the critics as a group. I mean the irrationally liberal ones. Renata Adler of the *The New York Times* almost foamed at the mouth because I showed a few massacres on the screen. She went into convulsions. She and other critics wouldn't believe that the Viet Cong are treacherous—that the dirty sons of bitches are raping, torturing gorillas. In the picture, I repeated the story General Stilwell told me about this South Vietnamese mayor. The V.C. tied him up and brought his wife out and about 40 men raped her, and then they brought out his two teenage daughters, hung them upside down and gutted them in front of him. And then they took an iron rod and beat his wife until every bone in her goddamn body was broken. That's torture, I'd say. So I mentioned this in the picture, and the critics were up in arms about that.

*PLAYBOY*: Did their comments jeopardize the financial success of the film?

*WAYNE*: Oh, God, no—they ensured it. Luckily for me, they overkilled it. *The Green Berets* would have been successful regardless of what the critics did, but it might have taken the public longer to find out about the picture if they hadn't made so much noise about it.

*PLAYBOY*: Did you resent the critics who labeled it a shameless propaganda film?

*WAYNE*: I agreed with them. It was an American film about American boys who were heroes over there. In that sense, it *was* propaganda.

*PLAYBOY*: Did you have any difficulties getting *The Green Berets* produced by a major studio?

*WAYNE*: A lot of them. Universal said they wanted to make the picture and we made a deal. Then the boys went to work on the head of Universal.

*PLAYBOY*: What boys?

*WAYNE*: The liberals. I don't know their names. But all of a sudden Universal changed its mind. They said, "This is an unpopular war." And I said, "What war was ever popular? You've already made the deal." Then they started saying, "Well, we don't want you to direct"—trying to use that as an excuse. So I said, "Well, screw this." So I let them renege and I just walked out. In an hour, I'd made another deal with Warner Bros., which was in the process of being sold to Seven Arts. Meanwhile, the guy at Universal couldn't keep his mouth shut. I let him off the hook, but he started blasting in the *Hollywood Reporter* that the picture couldn't make any money. I didn't go to the press and say these bastards backed out of a deal, but later—after Warner Bros.-Seven

Arts released it—I was very happy to inform Universal of the picture's success.

PLAYBOY: *The Alamo* was another of your patriotic films. What statement did this picture make?

WAYNE: I thought it would be a tremendous epic picture that would say "America."

PLAYBOY: Borden Chase, the screenwriter, has been quoted as saying, "When *The Alamo* was coming out, the word of mouth on it was that it was a dog. This was created by the Communists to get at Wayne. Then there were some bad reviews inspired by the Communists. . . . It's a typical Communist technique and they were using it against Duke for what he did in the early Fifties at the Motion Picture Alliance for the Preservation of American Ideals." Is that true?

WAYNE: Well, there's always a little truth in everything you hear. The Alliance thing was used pretty strongly against me in those days.

PLAYBOY: Was the Motion Picture Alliance formed to black list Communists and Communist sympathizers?

WAYNE: Our organization was just a group of motion-picture people on the right side, not leftist and not Commies. I was the president for a couple of years. There was no black list at that time, as some people said. That was a lot of horseshit. Later on, when Congress passed some laws making it possible to take a stand against these people, we were asked about Communists in the industry. So we gave them the facts as we knew them. That's all. The only thing our side did that was anywhere near black listing was just running a lot of people out of the business.

PLAYBOY: That sounds a good deal worse than black listing. Why couldn't you permit all points of view to be expressed freely on the screen?

WAYNE: Because it's been proven that communism is foreign to the American way of life. If you'd read the official Communist doctrine and then listened to the arguments of these people we were opposing, you'd find they were reciting propaganda by rote. Besides, these Communist sympathizers ran a lot of *our* people out of the business. One of them was a Pulitzer Prize winner who's now a columnist—Morrie Ryskind. They just never used him again at MGM after Dore Schary took charge of the studio, even though he was under contract.

*PLAYBOY*: What was the mood in Hollywood that made it so fashionable to take such a vigorous stand against communism?

*WAYNE*: Many of us were being invited to supposed social functions or house parties—usually at well-known Hollywood writers' homes—that turned out to be Communist recruitment meetings. Suddenly, everybody from make-up men to stagehands found themselves in seminars on Marxism. Take this colonel I knew, the last man to leave the Philippines on a submarine in 1942. He came back here and went to work sending food and gifts to U.S. prisoners on Bataan. He'd already gotten a Dutch ship that was going to take all this stuff over. The State Department pulled him off of it and sent the poor bastard out to be the technical director on my picture *Back to Bataan*, which was being made by Eddie Dmytryk. I knew that he and whole group of actors in the picture were pro-Reds, and when I wasn't there, these pro-Reds went to work on the colonel. He was a Catholic, so they kidded him about his religion. They even sang the *Internationale* at lunchtime. He finally came to me and said, "Mr. Wayne, I haven't anybody to turn to. These people are doing everything in their power to belittle me." So I went to Dmytryk and said, "Hey, are you a Commie?" He said, "No, I'm not a Commie. My father was a Russian. I was born in Canada. But if the masses of the American people want communism, I think it'd be good for our country." When he used the word "masses," he exposed himself. That word is not a part of Western terminology. So I knew he was a Commie. Well, it later came out that he was.

I also knew two other fellas who really did things that were detrimental to our way of life. One of them was Carl Foreman, the guy who wrote the screenplay for *High Noon*, and the other was Robert Rossen, the one who made the picture about Huey Long, *All the King's Men*. In Rossen's version of *All the King's Men*, which he sent me to read for a part, every character who had any responsibility at all was guilty of some offense against society. To make Huey Long a wonderful, rough pirate was great; but, according to this picture, everybody was a shit except for this weakling intern doctor who was trying to find a place in the world. I sent the script back to Charlie Feldman, my agent, and said, "If you ever send me a script like this again, I'll fire you." Ironically, it won the Academy Award.

*High Noon* was even worse. Everybody says *High Noon* is a great picture because Tiomkin wrote some great music for it and because Gary Cooper and Grace Kelly were in it. So it's got everything going for it. In that picture, four guys come in to gun down the sheriff. He goes to the church and asks for help and the guys go, "Oh well, oh gee." And the women stand up and say, "You're rats. You're rats. You're rats." So Cooper goes out alone. It's the most un-American thing I've ever seen in my whole life. The last thing in the picture is ole Coop putting the United States marshal's badge under his foot and stepping on it. I'll never regret having helped run Foreman out of this country.

*PLAYBOY*: What gave you the right?

*WAYNE*: Running him out of the country is just a figure of speech. But I did tell him that I thought he'd hurt Gary Cooper's reputation a great deal. Foreman said, "Well, what if I went to England?" I said, "Well, that's your business." He said, "Well, that's where I'm going." And he did.

*PLAYBOY*: You seem to have a very blunt way of dealing with people. Why?

*WAYNE*: I've always followed my father's advice: He told me, first, to always keep my word and, second, to never insult anybody unintentionally. If I insult you, you can be goddamn sure I intend to. And, third, he told me not to go around looking for trouble.

*PLAYBOY*: Don't you sometimes stray from these three tenets—particularly from the third one?

*WAYNE*: Well, I guess I have had some problems sticking to that third rule, but I'd say I've done pretty damn well with the first and second. I try to have good enough taste to insult only those I wish to insult. I've worked in a business where it's almost a requirement to break your word if you want to survive, but whenever I signed a contract for five years or for a certain amount of money, I've always lived up to it. I figured that if I was silly enough to sign it, or if I thought it was worth while at the time, that's the way she goes. I'm not saying that I won't drive as hard a bargain as I can. In fact, I think more about that end of the business than I did before, ever since 1959, when I found that my business manager was playing more than he was working. I didn't know how bad my financial condition was until my lawyer and somebody else said, "Let's all have a meeting and figure out exactly where you stand." At the conclusion of that meeting, it was quite obvious that I wasn't in anywhere near the shape that I thought I was or ought to be after 25 years of hard work. If they'd given me the time to sell everything without taking a quick loss, I would have come out about even.

*PLAYBOY*: Were you involved in money-losing deals?

*WAYNE*: Yeah. Oil and everything else. Not enough constructive thinking had been done. Then there was the shrimp fiasco. One of my dearest friends was Robert Arias, who was married to the ballerina Dame Margot Fonteyn. While his brother Tony was alive, we had control of about 70 percent of the shrimp in Panama. We were also buying some island property near the Panama Canal. We were going to put in a ship-repair place. There were tugs standing down there at $150 dollars a day to drag ships back up the United States, because repair prices in the Canal Zone were so high. But our plans fell through when Tony was killed in an airplane accident. Around a half a million dollars was lost.

*PLAYBOY*: Has your financial condition improved since then?

*WAYNE*: If anything happened to me now, I have the right amount of insurance, I hope and pray, for my estate. I'm about as big a rancher as there is in Arizona, so I have outside interests other than my motion-picture work. The turning point was the moment I decided to watch what was being done with my money.

*PLAYBOY*: Another—and certainly more dramatic—turning point for you was your cancer operation in 1964. At the time, were you optimistic about the outcome of the surgery?

*WAYNE*: Well, I had two operations six days apart—one for a cancer that was as big as a baby's fist, and then one for edema. I wasn't so uptight when I was told about the cancer. My biggest fear came when they twisted my windpipe and had to sew me back together a second time. When my family came in to see me and I saw the looks on their faces, I figured, "Well, Jeez, I must be just about all through."

*PLAYBOY*: How did you keep your spirits up?

*WAYNE*: By thinking about God and my family and my friends and telling myself, "Everything will be all right." And it was. I licked the big C. I know the man upstairs will pull the plug when he wants to, but I don't want to end up my life being sick. I want to go out on two feet—in action.

*PLAYBOY*: Does the loss of one lung restrict you from doing those rough-house movie stunts?

*WAYNE*: The operation hasn't impeded anything except that I get short of breath quickly. Particularly in the higher altitudes, that slows me down. I still do my own fights and all that stuff. I'd probably do a little bit more if I had the wind, but I still do more than my share. Nobody else does anything any more than I do, whether they're young or old.

*PLAYBOY*: Is it a matter of *machismo* for you to continue fighting your own fights?

*WAYNE*: I don't have to assert my virility. I think my career has shown that I'm not exactly a pantywaist. But I do take pride in my work, even to the point of being the first one on the set in the morning. I'm a professional.

*PLAYBOY*: In recent years, you've fallen off horses rather unprofessionally on a couple of occasions—once dislocating a shoulder during the production of *The Undefeated*. Wasn't that embarrassing?

*WAYNE*: What the hell, in my racket I've fallen off a lot of horses. I even fell off on purpose in *True Grit*. But that fall in *The Undefeated* was irritating because I tore some ligaments in my shoulder. I don't have good use of one arm anymore, and it makes me look like an idiot when I'm getting on a horse.

*PLAYBOY*: Is that an unfamiliar experience?

*WAYNE*: Getting on a horse?

*PLAYBOY*: Looking like an idiot?

*WAYNE*: Not hardly. One of the times I really felt like a fool was when I working on my first important film, *The Big Trail*, in Yuma, Arizona. I was three weeks flat on my back with *turistas*—or Montezuma's revenge, or the Aztec two-step, whatever you want to call it. You know, you get a little grease and soap on the inside of a fork and you've got it. Anyway, that was the worst case I ever had in my life. I'd been sick for so long that they finally said, "Jeez, Duke, if you can't get up now, we've got to get somebody else to take your place." So, with a loss of 18 pounds, I returned to work. My first scene was carrying in an actor named Tully Marshall, who was known to booze it up quite a bit. He had a big jug in his hand in this scene, and I set him down and we have a drink with another guy. They passed the jug to me first, and I dug back into it; it was straight rotgut bootleg whiskey. I'd been puking and crapping blood for a week and now I just poured that raw stuff right down my throat. After the scene, you can bet I called him every kind of an old bastard.

*PLAYBOY*: You've long been known for your robust drinking habits, whether it's rotgut bootleg or imported Scotch. How great is your capacity?

*WAYNE*: Well, I'm full grown, you know. I'm pretty big and got enough fat on me, so I guess I can drink a fair amount.

*PLAYBOY*: What kind of liquor has provided your most memorable hangovers?

*WAYNE*: *Conmemorativo* tequila. That's as fine a liquor as there is in the world. Christ, I tell you it's better than any whiskey; it's better than any schnapps; it's better than any drink I ever had in my life. You hear about tequila and think about a cheap cactus drink, but this is something extraordinary.

*PLAYBOY*: Many people argue that alcohol may be a more dangerous health hazard than marijuana. Would you agree?

*WAYNE*: There's been no top authority saying what marijuana does to you. I really don't know that much about it. I tried it once, but it didn't do anything to me. The kids say it makes them think they're going 30 miles an hour when they're going 80. If that's true, marijuana use should definitely be stopped.

*PLAYBOY*: Have you had any other experience with illegal drugs?

*WAYNE*: When I went to Hong Kong, I tried opium once, as a clinical thing. I heard it didn't make you sick the first time, and Jesus, it just didn't affect me one way or the other, either. So I'm not a very good judge of how debasing it is.

*PLAYBOY*: Do you think such drugs are debasing?

*WAYNE*: It's like water against a cliff. Each wave deteriorates it a little more. I'm quite sure that's the same thing that happens to human beings when they get hooked on drugs. What bothers me more is society's attitude toward drugs. We allowed all the hippies to stay together in Haight-Ashbury and turn it into a dirty, filthy, unattractive place. We allow the glorifying of drugs in our business—like in *Easy Rider*, where the guy says, "Jesus, don't you smoke pot?"—as if smoking pot is the same as chewing Bull Durham.

*PLAYBOY*: You chew tobacco, don't you?

*WAYNE*: I learned to do that in college. During football season, when we couldn't smoke, we always used to chew. When I was a kid, if you wore a new pair of shoes, everybody would spit on them. I haven't practiced spitting lately, so don't wear your new shoes and expect me to hit them with any accuracy. I'm not the marksman I used to be.

*PLAYBOY*: You chew, but you don't use drugs. Do you still have as much drink, food and sex as you used to?

*WAYNE*: I drink as much as I ever did. I eat more than I should. And my sex life is none of your goddamn business.

*PLAYBOY*: Sexuality, however, seems a large part of your magnetism. According to one Hollywood writer, "Wayne has a sexual authority so strong that even a child could perceive it." Do you feel you still convey that onscreen?

*WAYNE*: Well, at once time in my career, I guess sexuality was part of my appeal. But God, I'm 63 years old now. How the hell do I know whether I still convey that? Jeez. It's pretty hard to answer a question like, "Are you attractive to broads?" All that crap comes from the way I walk, I guess. There's evidently a virility in it. Otherwise, why do they keep mentioning it? But I'm certainly not conscious of any particular walk. I guess I must walk different than other people, but I haven't gone to any school to learn how.

*PLAYBOY*: Another integral ingredient of your image is a rugged manliness, a readiness to mix up with anyone who gets in your way. Have you ever run into situations in a restaurant or a bar in which someone tried to pick a fight with you?

*WAYNE*: It never happens to me anymore. Whatever my image is, it's friendly. But there was one time, a number of years ago, that I did get a little irritated. I was wearing long hair—the exception then, not the rule—and I was, if I say so myself, a fairly handsome kid. Anyway, I'm dancing with my wife-to-be and I'm saying to her quietly, "You're beautiful enough to marry." Some punk alongside pipes up, "Forget about him, lady; not with that hair." So I sat her down and went over and explained very gently to him that if he would step outside, I'd kick his fuckin' teeth down his throat. That ended that.

PLAYBOY: Having once worn long hair yourself, how do you feel about long-haired young people?

WAYNE: They don't bother me. If a guy wants to wear his hair down to his ass, I'm not revolted by it. But I don't look at him and say, "Now there's a fella I'd like to spend next winter with."

PLAYBOY: Who *would* you like to spend time with?

WAYNE: That's easy. Winston Churchill. He's the most terrific fella of our century. If I had to make a speech on the subject of communism, I could think of nobody that had a better insight or that said things concerning the future that have proven out so well. Let me read to you from a book of his quotes. While Roosevelt was giving the world communism, Churchill said, "I tell you—it's no use arguing with a Communist. It's no good trying to convert a Communist, or persuade him. You can only deal with them on the following basis . . . you can only do it by having superior force on your side on the matter in question—and they must also be convinced that you will use—you will not hesitate to use—these forces if necessary, in the most ruthless manner.

"You have not only to convince the Soviet government that you have superior force—but that you are not restrained by any moral consideration if the case arose from using that force with complete material ruthlessness. And that is the greatest chance of peace, the surest road to peace." Churchill was unparalleled. Above all, he took a nearly beaten nation and kept their dignity for them.

PLAYBOY: Many pessimists insist that our nation has lost its dignity and is headed toward self-destruction. Some, in fact, compare the condition of our society to the decline and fall of the Roman Empire and the last days of Sodom and Gomorrah. Are you that gloomy about the future of America?

WAYNE: Absolutely not. I think that the loud roar of irresponsible liberalism, which in the old days we called radicalism, is being quieted down by a reasoning public. I think the pendulum's swinging back. We're remembering that the past can't be so bad. We built a nation on it. We must also look always to the future. Tomorrow—the time that gives a man or a country just one more chance—is just one of many things that I feel are wonderful in life. So's a good horse under you. Or the only campfire for miles around. Or a quiet night and a nice soft hunk of ground to sleep on. Or church bells sending out their invitations. A mother meeting her first-born. The sound of a kid calling you Dad for the first time. There's a lot of things great about life. But I think tomorrow is the most important thing. Comes in to us at midnight very clean, ya know. It's perfect when it arrives and it puts itself in our hands. It hopes we've learned something from yesterday. As a country, our yesterdays tell us that we have to win not only at war but at peace. So far we haven't done that. Sadly, it looks like we'll have to win another war to win a peace. All I can hope is that in our anxiety to have peace, we remember our clear and present dangers and beware the futility of compromise; only if we keep sight of both will we have a chance of stumbling forward into a day when there won't be guns fired anymore in anger.

*PLAYBOY*: Contrasting the America you grew up in and the America of today, is it the same kind of country, or has it changed?

*WAYNE*: The only difference I can see is that we now have an enemy within our borders fighting with propaganda and coloring events in a manner that belittles our great country. But all in all, it's practically the same.

*PLAYBOY*: In retrospect, would you have wanted your life to have been any different?

*WAYNE*: If I had it to do over again, I'd probably do everything I did. But that's not necessarily the right thing to do.

*PLAYBOY*: What legacy do you hope to leave behind?

*WAYNE*: Well, you're going to think I'm being corny, but this is how I really feel: I hope my family and my friends will be able to say that I was an honest, kind and fairly decent man.

# NOTES

1. Wayne gives himself an Oscar nomination for *She Wore a Yellow Ribbon* that he never received and characterizes his rowdy role in *Allegheny Uprising* as "cautious."

2. See discussion of interviews in chapter 4.

3. Released under the title *Big Jake* in 1971.

4. This figure is questionable; see my remarks preceding Wayne's filmography in appendix A.

# 4

# BIBLIOGRAPHICAL ESSAY

The course of John Wayne's career and his significance in American culture have been treated by many writers in many forms. The descriptive bibliographical essay that follows cannot discuss in detail the great quantity of published materials about Wayne, particularly in the popular press, but it does cover the books, interviews, scholarly and critical articles, and miscellaneous print sources. The next chapter on information sources provides full citations for all sources cited in this book and, additionally, lists popular and fan magazine articles, nonprint materials, and archival resources.

## BOOKS

### Biographies and Books about Wayne

Film star biographies are notoriously lightweight; half old newspaper stories and half speculation. Although many of these books conform to that type, value can be found in most.

Most biographies published before Wayne's death give little space to his negative qualities. An exception, and the most substantial of the biographies as a whole, is Maurice Zolotow's *Shooting Star: A Biography of John Wayne* (1974; rev. ed. 1979).

Although he includes no formal documentation, Zolotow credits a wide range of sources, including interviews of Wayne friends, family, and associates. The book is detailed, largely objective, and written in a clear style. Zolotow avoids typical excesses of style, bias, and fabrication. Others don't avoid them. Mike Tomkies's *Duke: The Real Story of John Wayne* (1971) has little ill to say about Wayne, offering what has become the standard version of his life and career. The treatment of Wayne's life in George Carpozi's *The John Wayne Story* (1972; rev. ed. 1979) is slapdash—some solid detail, lots of embroidery. He seems determined to make John Wayne an event in his life, so episodes are often framed as "when I heard," "when my wife read me a review," and so on. Carpozi does have lots of detail, pulling together news coverage of Wayne into a narrative, and the revised edition provides an account of Wayne's last days and funeral. *Duke: The Real Story of John Wayne* (1973; rev. ed. 1979) by Jean Ramer provides little if any information that is not found elsewhere, and Ramer's approach both glorifies and sensationalizes Wayne's personality and career. An unusual biography for children, casting Wayne as American-cowboy-hero, also appeared in the late seventies: *John Wayne* by Richard Whittingham (1977). The last biography to appear before Wayne's death, George Bishop's *John Wayne: The Actor/The Man* (1979), is a very uneven book, badly written with questionable use of the few sources credited. Bishop's own sexist and right-wing politics flavor many critical assessments of Wayne, but he offers some good discussions of his growth as an actor. In these sections, too, Bishop proposes intriguing connections between Wayne as a private person and as a screen persona.

Three books published in the eighties give perspectives and information different from the earlier ones. Wayne's secretary and last romantic "companion," Pat Stacy, covers her time with him in *Duke: A Love Story. An Intimate Memoir of John Wayne's Last Years* (1983). Here can be found valuable facts about Wayne's business and family relationships during the last years, flavored, of course, by Stacy's personal involvement. Balanced against

Stacy's book is a biography by Wayne's widow, Pilar Wayne's *John Wayne: My Life with the Duke* (1987). She covers familiar territory, adding little new material about most of his life, but the book is useful in providing details of their life together and the family relationships as she sees them. Finally, *Duke: The Life and Times of John Wayne*, by Donald Shepherd and Robert Slatzer with Dave Grayson (1985), also offers an intimate's view of Wayne. (Grayson was his personal makeup man for fifteen years.) This biography adds substantially to the documentation of Wayne's life; the authors acknowledge the difficulty of locating primary sources and the problems of verifying secondary ones. Unlike other books, thus, they name sources and provide chapter notes. Often, they "correct" a longstanding version of some facet of Wayne's life on the basis of these sources. They provide new facts of his childhood and extensive detail of his last years. Most valuable, perhaps, is the vivid portrait of the actor's arrogance, temper, and generosity which emerges from on-the-job anecdotes. This book, combined with Zolotow's, gives the most complete record of Wayne's life.[1]

Other books cover Wayne's life and career primarily in a coffee table photo-book format. The best of these is *Duke: The John Wayne Album* by John Boswell and Jay David (1979). A personal and career history rich in anecdotal detail, the book depends on earlier accounts and newspaper clippings, but the compilation is smooth. Illustrations are good and range from shots of Glendale, California, as it was when Wayne moved there as a boy to a full color spread on Wayne posters and comic books. It also provides handy boxed features of tidbits: lists of sports films he made, non-Wayne films he produced, quotes on acting, and so on. Also solid as a photo-book treatment of Wayne's career is *John Wayne: A Tribute* by Norm Goldstein (1979). A wide range of professional and newspaper stills cover Wayne's public life. Sam Shaw's *John Wayne in the Camera Eye* (1979) presents an album of good family and on-location shots, along with a brief account of life and career. Others in this category: *The Life and Times of John Wayne* (1979); *John Wayne* by Philippe Ferrari (in French, 1980);

*John Wayne* (E-Go Series, 1976); *The John Wayne Scrapbook* by
Lee Pfeiffer (1989); and *The Official John Wayne Reference Book*
by Charles John Kiesat (1985).


## Filmographies

Almost all of the biographies of Wayne have filmographies, in
that they list his films with brief credits. There are, however, two
good book-length filmographies. *John Wayne* by Allen Eyles
(1976; rev. ed. 1979) is indispensable for extensive study of
Wayne's films. It contains a film-by-film discussion of his career
with lots of stills, detailed synopses, and brief critical assessments. Although small details of dialogue and action are occa-
sionally inaccurate, the summaries capture the essential plot and
flavor of each film. Eyles critiques with a sure eye, also, placing
films and individual roles in the context of Wayne's developing
career. The opening chapters look at his image ("God Loves John
Wayne") and his professional stature ("Working with Wayne").
A reprint of a Scott Eyman interview and a section of color shots
were added for the 1979 "memorial edition." Most valuable,
perhaps, is the very detailed filmography which closes out the
book. All films, including those for which Wayne did a walk-on
or other minor work are listed with U.S. and British titles,
directors, writers, cinematographers, editors, producers, distrib-
utors, art directors, music, running time, color process, full cast
list, release dates in U.S. and Britain, and information on remakes
or reissues.

Another valuable filmography is *The Films of John Wayne* by
Mark Ricci and Boris and Steve Zmijewsky (1970; rev. ed. 1979).
A short biographical-critical discussion of Wayne's image opens
the book, but most important is the film listing, which gives stills,
full cast, credits for director, writer, cinematographer, editor, art
director, music, sound, running time, release dates, and brief plot
synopsis for each film. (Because of their brevity, these synopses
have less range for error and thus fewer inaccuracies than Eyles'

do. Eyles' book gives more information in the long run, of course.)

Others are *Starring John Wayne* by Gene Fernett (1969) and *John Wayne: Le Dernier Géant* by Francois Pascal, with Francois Guerif and Pascal Merigeau (1980), which is a full filmography in French.

## Books about Stars

Many compilations of pictures and/or short discussions of star personalities have been published; John Wayne appears in most. The nature of these books allows for superficial analysis of the star's image and contribution to film. Most touch with little substance on Wayne as a star; as a whole, however, they provide some insight into the formation of Wayne's image.

The most superficial are the oversize picture-books, which usually include a page of commentary and a handful of stills. These picture-books are typical: David Castell's *Superstars of the 1970's* (1974), Richard Griffith's *The Movie Stars* (1970), John Kobal's *Fifty Superstars* (1974), James Robert Parish's *Great Movie Heroes* (1975), Danny Peary's *Closeups: The Movie Star Book* (1978), Richard Schickel and Allen Hurlburt's *The Stars: Personalities Who Made the Movies,* and Elisabeth Weis's *The National Society of Film Critics on the Movie Star* (1981) (which reprints Jack Kroll's *Newsweek* obituary of Wayne).

Another variety of picture-book covers stars of a popular genre, in Wayne's case, the western or war picture. Examples are Ernest Corneau's *The Hall of Fame of Western Stars* (1969) and Lee O. Miller's *The Great Cowboy Stars of Movies and Westerns* (1979). Gene Fernett has done two books on B movies which include Wayne's work, *Next Time Drive Off the Cliff!*, and *Poverty Row* (1973).

Probably the most interesting, and sometimes useful, compilations about stars are the gossip books, where insiders or the stars themselves share stories about Hollywood life. Wayne comes up in Alan Barbour's *A Thousand and One Delights* (1971), Ezra

Goodman's *The Fifty-Year Decline and Fall of Hollywood* (1961), Phil Hirsch's *Hollywood Uncensored* (1965), Joe Hyams's *Mislaid in Hollywood* (1973), and Jane Wilkie's *Confessions of an Ex-Fan Magazine Writer* (1981). In *Gone Hollywood* (1979), Christopher Finch and Linda Rosenkrantz include Paul Fix's account of coaching Wayne how to move gracefully. Wayne discusses his acting in Charles Hamblett's *The Hollywood Cage* (1966, 1969). In *The Whole Truth and Nothing But* (1963), gossip columnist Hedda Hopper assesses Wayne's anticommunist politics. *Hello Hollywood!* (1962) by Allen Rivkin and Laura Kerr contains the most about Wayne: a reprint of a *Look* interview and a study of Wayne at work on *The Barbarian and the Geisha*.

Finally, a few works analyze stars and stardom more critically. Edgar Morin's *The Stars* (1957; trans. 1960) and Alexander Walker's *Stardom: The Hollywood Phenomenon* (1970) both feature Wayne; in particular, Walker devotes a chapter to him as a political star. *Stars* by Richard Dyer (1979) is a ground-breaking study of methodology for the study of actors/stars. Dyer cites Wayne's career and image as representative in several sections, and constructs an especially interesting semiotic analysis of Wayne's acting technique.

### Biographies of Others

Because of his long career, Wayne figured in the lives of hundreds of Hollywood people. Many of their biographies and autobiographies offer anecdotes of his professional and personal lives, rarely more than three or four pages long, often only in passing references. Wayne's biographers have culled most of the longer stories from these books, but many are worth reading in context to understand the flavor of the relationship with Wayne or to gain a full sense of the making of a Wayne film. A number of biographies make brief mention of John Wayne; those discussed here have unusual or substantive material.

Most informative are books about directors. In an extensive interview section of Peter Bogdanovich's *Allen Dwan: The Last*

*Pioneer* (1971), the director Dwan comments significantly about working with Wayne in the making of *Sands of Iwo Jima*. Frank Capra, in his *The Name Above the Title: An Autobiography* (1971), explains about quitting as director of *Circus World* after conflict with Wayne's writers. In *Pappy: The Life of John Ford* (1979), Dan Ford, the director's grandson, retells the familiar Ford-Wayne stories and adds new ones. This biography fully portrays the male camaraderie of Ford, Wayne, Ward Bond, Grant Withers, and others. Andrew Sinclair's *John Ford* (1979) also features the usual Ford-Wayne stories in detail. Wayne's work with Marlene Dietrich in an early film, *Seven Sinners*, is recounted by its director, Tay Garnett in his autobiography, *Light Your Torches and Pull Up Your Tights* (1973). John Huston's *An Open Book* (1980) explains what went wrong in making *The Barbarian and the Geisha*, faulting Wayne, while Axel Madsen's *John Huston* (1978) details more objectively the production of that film. An account of work on *Cast A Giant Shadow* in Melville Shavelson's *How to Make a Jewish Movie* (1971) describes Wayne's contribution in favorable terms. And William Wellman, the director of several 1950's Wayne films, speaks fondly of that work and documents Wayne's power as a producer in *A Short Time for Insanity* (1974). In *Each Man in His Time: The Life Story of a Director* (1974), Raoul Walsh, who gave Wayne his first big part, recounts how Wayne was chosen for *The Big Trail* and how he got his name.

Others besides directors have given valuable accounts of working with Wayne. Stuntman Yakima Canutt, in *Stunt Man* (1979), details his work in Wayne films, but with little insight into the man as co-worker. On the other hand, Chuck Roberson, a stuntman who was Wayne's double for years, tells many colorful anecdotes of working with him. Wayne's contributions to films and his relationship with John Ford are also depicted in Roberson's *The Fall Guy: 30 Years as the Duke's Double* (1980). In *Starmaker: The Autobiography of Hal Wallis* (1980), Wallis, the producer of *True Grit* and *Rooster Cogburn*, explains their conception and Wayne's role in their making. And actor Robert

Stack tells stories of political and professional moments shared
with Wayne in his autobiography, *Straight Shooting* (1980).

## Critical Studies

A wide range of book-length studies treat John Wayne as actor,
star, or public figure. Although some works cover several aspects,
the books can be grouped: those about his films, about film genres
he dominated, about the work of his major directors, and about
his cultural image.

Specific Wayne films receive detailed attention in a handful of
books. *Stagecoach* is well-documented in Richard J. Anobile's
*John Ford's Stagecoach Starring John Wayne* (1975), a virtual
shot-by-shot reproduction of the film, valuable as a tool in
examining Wayne's physical presence on the screen. This book
also includes a reprint of an *Action* interview of Ford concerning
the film. The interview is also reprinted in *Directors in ACTION*
(1973), edited by Bob Thomas. This collection contains a long
section on *Stagecoach*, including reminiscences by Wayne, Claire
Trevor, and others. The screen play of *Stagecoach* by Dudley
Nichols can be found in *Twenty Best Film Plays* (1943), edited
by John Gassner and Dudley Nichols. A 1971 edition edited by
Nicola Hayden also includes Nichols's source, a short story by
Ernest Haycox. Two books address quite different aspects of *The
Alamo*, the project Wayne starred in, directed, and produced. In
*The Real Oscar: The Story Behind the Academy Awards* (1981),
Peter H. Brown details the publicity campaign Wayne (and others)
waged for the film. Richard Maltby's *Harmless Entertainment:
Hollywood and the Ideology of Consensus* (1983) devotes a
section to *The Alamo* as an example of film as commodity, and
thoughtfully considers how Wayne dominates the narrative of his
films. Kevin Brownlow's beautifully illustrated *The War, the West
and the Wilderness* (1979) includes *The Big Trail*. In a chapter
of *Twenty-Four Frames a Second* (1970) entitled "John Ford: A
Persistence of Vision," William S. Pechter attributes meaning in
*The Man Who Shot Liberty Valance* to Wayne's iconographic

image and provides a valuable study of the entire film. William Meyer, in *The Making of the Great Westerns* (1979), provides synopses and production details for *Stagecoach, Red River, Fort Apache, Rio Bravo, El Dorado,* and *True Grit.* Several films are touched on in William Froug's *The Screen Writer Looks at the Screenwriter* (1972), in that screenwriters who worked on Wayne's films are interviewed; notable is William Bowers' account of an encounter with a drunken Wayne, who had wanted Bowers' property, *The Gunfighter.* And finally, in *America in the Movies or "Santa Maria, It Had Slipped My Mind"* (1975), Michael Wood's impressionistic analysis uses lesser Wayne films as interesting examples of themes in American film (*The Spoilers, The Undefeated*).

Wayne's films and his work as an actor are also examined in books about directors of those films, notably John Ford and Howard Hawks, whose direction shaped his career and image. Most studies of Ford assume an auteur stance for analysis and focus on the director's work, with Wayne as a static element, more than a contributing artist. But detailed attention to important Wayne films gives value to such studies; among them are *The Cinema of John Ford* (1971) by John Baxter, *Authorship and Narrative in the Cinema* (1977) by William Luhr and Peter Lehman, *The Western Films of John Ford* (1974) and *The Non-Western Films of John Ford* (1979) by J. A. Place, and *About John Ford* (1981) by Lindsay Anderson. Best of the lot is *John Ford* (1975) by Joseph McBride and Michael Wilmington, for its sensible discussion of Ford's themes and genres and for including Wayne's contribution to both. Peter Bogdanovich's *John Ford* (1967; rev. ed. 1978) differs somewhat. A compilation of personal essays on Ford, accompanied by a long interview and thorough filmography, this book is packed with isolated details about Wayne's working relationship with Ford.

Books about Howard Hawks analyze Wayne's contribution to the films in more substantive fashion than do those about Ford. These books examine Wayne as a Hawks actor: *The Hollywood Professionals: Howard Hawks, Frank Borzage, Edgar G. Ulmer*

(1974) by John Belton, *Die Kamera in Augenhohe: Begegnungen Mit Howard Hawks* (1979) by Hans C. Blumenberg, and *Focus on Howard Hawks* (1972) edited by Joseph McBride. Donald C. Willis's *The Films of Howard Hawks* (1975) covers all of the Wayne films and includes a long interview of Hawks which details their work together.

Of less value are books about other Wayne directors giving some details, but little analysis, of Wayne's work: *John Ford and Andrew V. McLaglen* (1970) by Michael Burrows, *The Men Who Made the Movies* (1975) (interviews of Walsh, Hawks, Wellman) by Richard Schickel, and *The Hollywood Professionals: Michael Curtiz, Raoul Walsh, and Henry Hathaway* (1973) by Kingsley Canham.

Wayne dominated the war and western film genres, so most analyses of these address his contribution. One stands above the rest in its quality of research and analysis: Lawrence Suid's *Guts and Glory: Great American War Movies* (1978). This valuable study devotes two chapters to Wayne, covering *Sands of Iwo Jima*, *The Green Berets*, and Wayne's image as *the* American military hero. Suid interviewed film and military personnel on these films, so he provides information about the alliance between Hollywood and the Pentagon, in addition to Wayne's place in the genre. Norman Kagan's *The War Film* (1974) touches on several of Wayne's war films, but analyzes in depth only *The Green Berets*, noting the film's underlying cynicism. In *Looking Away: Hollywood and Vietnam* (1975), Julian Smith offers an unsympathetic study of Wayne and *The Green Berets* in relation to the war itself.

Many books about westerns include Wayne's work. Superficial picture-book collections emphasize Wayne's place in the genre, but provide little analysis of the significance of his work. Typical of these are Walter Clapham's *Western Movies* (1974), Eric Warman and Tom Vallance's *Westerns: A Preview Special* (1964), and George Fenin and William K. Everson's *The Western: From Silents to the Seventies* (1973). A few books study the history of the western, placing Wayne in context. Two histories deal with the serials and B westerns in which he began his career. Alan

Barbour's *The Thrill of It All* (1971) gives Wayne a chapter, mostly stills, in this account of the B's. *The Vanishing Legion: A History of Mascot Pictures, 1927-1935* (1981) by Jon Tuska covers Wayne's early career in considerable detail. Tuska's *The Filming of the West* (1976) emphasizes certain classic films, among them Wayne's *Stagecoach, The Dark Command, Red River, Rio Bravo, Fort Apache, She Wore A Yellow Ribbon, Hondo, McClintock, True Grit,* and *The Cowboys.* Several useful analyses of the forms and conventions of the Western feature Wayne. Philip French's *Westerns: Aspects of a Movie Genre* (1973; rev. ed. 1977) illustrates its analytical assertions with Wayne's roles. In particular, his late films are analyzed for themes of aging and the last of the West. *Focus on the Western* (1974), edited by Jack Nachbar, collects much of the good criticism of the genre; several essays deal with Wayne's work. A classic French study of the genre, containing several sections on Wayne's major directors, John Ford and Howard Hawks, is *La Grande Adventure du Western: Du Far West a Hollywood* (1964) by Jean-Louis Rieupeyrout. Charles Silver dedicates his book, *The Western Film* (1976), to Wayne and calls him "most important of all Western actors." His roles in key films are analyzed by Silver with similar bias. *Shooting Stars: Heroes and Heroines of Western Film* (1987) by Archie P. McDonald gives a chapter to Wayne with a sensible perspective and overview of his contribution.

Three studies of genres in Hollywood film, Stuart Kaminsky's *American Film Genres: Approaches to a Critical Theory of Popular Film* (1974), Stanley Solomon's *Beyond Formula: American Film Genres* (1976), and Thomas Schatz's *Hollywood Genres: Formulas, Filmmaking and the Studio System* (1981) all feature Wayne as part of an examination of the western. Each makes insightful observations about his place in the genre's evolution; Schatz's is the most substantive study. In a more complex look at film genre, *The World in A Frame* (1976), Leo Braudy discusses the films Wayne did for Ford and Hawks. Also, Wayne's acting style and role as an icon are touched on.

Other books examine the west and western hero in a cultural context beyond, but including, Wayne's film image. In Jenni Calder's *There Must Be a Lone Ranger: The American West in Film and in Reality* (1974), Wayne's identity as *the* western hero is assumed more than examined, and his films illustrate various themes Calder traces. The discussion of Wayne is rich in detail, but dependent on other sources. Robert V. Hine's *The American West: An Interpretative History* (1973) touches on Wayne's contribution to "The Cowboy and the Cult of Masculinity" and "The Western Hero." William W. Savage, Jr., in *The Cowboy Hero: His Image in American History and Culture* (1979), uses Wayne throughout as the foremost representative of the mythic cowboy, but offers limited analysis of what he signifies in that role. In the most valuable of these cultural studies, *Showdown: Confronting America in the Western Film* (1980), John H. Lenihan looks at Wayne's films and public image as they reflect American attitudes.

A handful of books examine Wayne's film image and cultural iconography in a broad context. An essay by Peter Bogdanovich in his *Pieces of Time* (1973) pays homage to Wayne as both actor and star. Alan G. Barbour's *John Wayne* (1974), as part of the Pyramid series, competently covers many topics, notably "The Image," "The Man," and "The Essential Wayne" (key roles). In *John Wayne: Prophet of the American Way of Life* (1988), Emanuel Levy provides cultural analysis of Wayne's life and films. Richard D. McGhee explores all facets in his interesting *John Wayne: Actor, Artist, Hero* (1990), including literary and mythic explanations of Wayne's persona. Frank McConnell sees Wayne as an Arthurian figure, representative of a lost epic world, in his *Storytelling and Mythmaking: Images from Film and Literature* (1979). Four writers explore Wayne's image as American male. Molly Haskell, in *From Reverence to Rape: Women in the Movies* (1974, rev. ed. 1987), considers Wayne in relation to women, especially as an appealing older man. Michael Malone's *Heroes of Eros: Male Sexuality in the Movies* (1979) superficially examines Wayne as male, while Joan Mellen, in

*Big Bad Wolves: Masculinity in the American Film* (1977), details her analysis. Like Haskell, Mellen sees Wayne as the prototypical "real" man in American film, but finds his male characters more likeable, emotionally variable, and genteel than macho types like Clint Eastwood. Donald Spoto analyzes male identity in *Camerado: Hollywood and the American Man* (1978), and sees Wayne as he appears in Hawks films as acting out masculine companionship.

## ARTICLES

Except for interviews of John Wayne, periodical articles are grouped here according to the type of publication in which they appear. The interviews, articles from film journals, and miscellaneous print are discussed in essay format. Because of their numbers, articles from popular magazines and fan magazines are listed in the next chapter without annotations. Newspaper articles are too numerous: a listing of press articles about Wayne would approach infinity. Indexes for *The New York Times*, *The Washington Post*, *The Los Angeles Times*, and papers of comparable size should be consulted. *The Los Angeles Times* index is particular useful because the paper covered Wayne as a local citizen as well as film star. Also, he often responded by letter to their articles about him. Indexes to newspapers in areas of the country where Wayne worked on location (e.g., Texas, Arizona, Seattle) and where he owned property or business interests (Washington, Arizona) are also valuable.

### Interviews

Interviews given by Wayne for popular magazines usually correspond to the opening of a new film; he answers questions in predictable, brief fashion. The articles themselves are short, in keeping with the limits of space in such publications. Typical of such interviews are "Did You Ever Think of Duke as Big Daddy?" by Edwin Miller for *Seventeen*, in which

Wayne talks of his career and America; *Ladies Home Journal*'s
"Wayne, Westerns, and Women" by Molly Haskell, conducted
on the set of *The Shootist*, in which he discusses women, aging,
and his power as a filmmaker; and M. Ronan's "Two Screen
Cowboys Talk About the Reel and the Real West" in *Senior
Scholastic*, which interviews Wayne and Ben Johnson. A few
others of this type cover little more than Wayne's image and
current film release: George Flatley's "Cowboy of Cop; Wayne
Never Wanes," Lorraine Gaugin's "Duke in Durango," Molly
Haskell's "What Makes John Wayne Larger Than Life," Roy
Litchtenstein's "Hey Mister! Wayne Marks First Fifty Years."
Peter Bogdanovich's homage to Wayne at his death, "Duke's
Gone West," compiles brief segments of past interviews. And
*The Saturday Evening Post* has published a series of tributes
to Wayne which included interviews by Pete Martin, "Ladies
Like 'em Rugged," and D. Sutton, "John Wayne: Image vs.
Man."

The most substantial interviews of Wayne appear in film
journals and magazines for men. In "Looking Back: John Wayne
Talking to Scott Eyman" in *Focus on Film*, Eyman quizzes Wayne
about his work with major directors, his assessment of some of
his films, his future plans, and his politics. Wayne's testy, brief
responses provide tantalizing detail about his work. F. A.
Macklin's long, rambling interview for *Film Heritage*, " 'I Come
Ready': An Interview with John Wayne," is very valuable for
insights into Wayne's expertise as a filmmaker and for its glimpse
of a mellow, polite side to his personality. In "John Wayne Talks
Tough" by Joe McInerney for *Film Comment*, the interviewer
leads Wayne over familiar territory (Ford, Hawks, his start in B
westerns), but also elicits comments on acting and directing.
Thomas B. Morgan's "God and Man in Hollywood" in *Esquire*
scrutinizes Wayne's image and its impact on American politics.
The *Playboy* editors' "Playboy Interview: John Wayne" offers
extensive questioning of Wayne about his life, work, image, and
politics: his responses are brash and candid. This interview is
reprinted in this book.

## Articles in Film Journals

The many articles about Wayne appearing in film journals may be grouped by their general subjects: filmography, work done with other filmmakers (including interviews of others), films and his meaning in them, and career history and resulting image. Useful information for the Wayne filmography, including some obscure items, is found in Karl Thiede's "John Wayne, A Comprehensive Filmography" and Jim Beaver's "John Wayne." Two items in *Classic Films Collection* add details, too: "Alternate Films Titles to John Wayne Films" and J. W. Mace's "John Wayne Rareties." In "John Wayne," W.-E. Buhler offers a bio-filmography of Wayne as a member of John Ford's "stock company."

A variety of articles cover Wayne as he worked with others in his films. "Comments on John Wayne" in *Film Heritage* quotes opinions of various co-workers and critics about Wayne (Strother Martin's is the most intriguing). Two interviews with Don Siegel, director of *The Shootist*, touch on Wayne as co-worker: Ralph Applebaum's "Making 'The Shootist': An Interview with Don Siegel" and T. Ockersen's " 'Ik ben net enn hoer die geen geld kan weest ann': interview met Don Siegel." In Jim Kitses' "The Rise and Fall of the American West: Borden Chase Interviewed," Chase, the screenwriter of *Red River*, recounts the writing of the film and working with Wayne to develop the character of Tom Dunson. Two interviews of the director Howard Hawks discuss several Wayne films: " 'Do I Get to Play the Drunk This Time?' " and "Hawks Talks: New Anecdotes from the Old Master" by Joseph McBride and Gerald Peary, in which Hawks denies Chase's account of the making of *Red River* and explains why he wouldn't work with Wayne again. Martin Gray's "No-Contract Star" discusses Wayne's roles for John Ford. Susan D'Arcy's "The Indestructibles" depicts Wayne and Katharine Hepburn happily working together, while J. Mariani's "John Wayne's Women" surveys his leading ladies in many films. Two articles in *American Cinematographer* offer accounts by men who shot Wayne films: Winston Hoch's "The Vietnam War as Filmed for

*The Green Berets"* and Herb A. Lightman's "Filming *The Alamo* in Todd AO." Wayne himself explains his work on *The Alamo* in "Why I Turned Producer and Director."

Specific Wayne films are examined closely in several articles, almost always with attention to how his presence or performance contributed meaning. In "Reflections on the Tradition of the Movie Western," Douglas Brode considers *Red River* as a parallel to *Moby Dick* and Wayne as its star. *Red River* is also the subject of Robert Sklar's "Empire to the West: *Red River*"; he discusses it as a political film and Wayne's character as expressing imperialist values. In "Beloved Husband and Father," T. Bendtsen looks at such themes in several films, especially *The Quiet Man.* Stuart Kaminsky's "Legend of the Lost" is notable for a close analysis of a minor Wayne film (*Legend of the Lost*), an argument for director Hathaway as auteur, and a contrast of Hathaway's use of Wayne to Ford's and Hawks's. Barbara Bernstein's "Not Likely" differs in its view of Hathaway. Arguing Wayne's performance lacks skill in *True Grit*, she faults Hathaway's direction as one reason. James V. D. Card compares novel and film in "*The Searchers*: by Alan LeMay and by John Ford" observing that Wayne's presence as Ethan Edwards lends the themes of racism and isolation more power in the film. A structural analysis of *Rio Lobo*, *El Dorado*, and *Rio Bravo* in Judith Bernstein's "The Valley of the Shadow" explores parallels and changes in Wayne roles in these Hawks westerns. Also, Richard T. Jameson, in "Talking and Doing in *Rio Bravo*," insightfully analyzes acting in this film, giving close attention to Wayne's performance. "*The Shootist*: redemption of discredited authority" by Stephen Albert looks at the political implications of Wayne's heroic persona. And in "Cactus Rosebud or The Man Who Shot Liberty Valance," while discussing *The Man Who Shot Liberty Valance* as a "memory film," Andrew Sarris posits that Wayne is an icon for the old West. Lawrence Suid has two articles concerned with *The Green Berets*. "Hollywood and Viet Nam" includes Wayne's comments on the film in a general survey of movies done on the war. "The Making of the Green Berets" is a very thorough account of the

Army's role in making the film. Suid interviewed producer Michael Wayne and had access to Batjac production files to document his work.

Several articles examine the course of Wayne's career, and many propose significant patterns emerge from his life and acting—patterns which explain his importance in American culture. Dennis Hall's "Tall in the Saddle" surveys, with some inaccuracies, all films through *The Undefeated*, with some analysis of Wayne heroes. In "Action Speaks Louder Than Dialogue," Tony Crawley considers the early action films done for Republic Studios. A valuable analysis of Wayne's acting in roles done for Ford and Hawks appears in John Belton's "John Wayne: As Sure as the Turning o' the Earth." Michael Budd, in "Genre, Director and Stars in John Ford's Westerns: Fonda, Wayne, Stewart and Widmark," also looks at the roles done for Ford, tracing the evolution of the Ford-Wayne hero as emblem of change in the West and the Western. Valerio Andrade's "O Ultimo Cowboy" examines Wayne as *the* western hero, with filmography. In "John Wayne: Hero with A Thousand Faces," Richard D. McGhee asserts important Wayne roles reflect Campbell's monomyth and Frye's cyclic view of genre. Wayne roles are variously categorized in Anne-Marie Bidault's "John Wayne et ses Mythologies: Un Grand Géant au Beret Vert." She discusses him as epic hero, imperialist hero, man of mission, good bad man, American historical figure, Irishman, and man of violence, also with filmography. Similarly, Andrew Sinclair, in "Man on Horseback: The Seven Faces of John Wayne," combines Wayne's screen and off-screen images to identify his "faces": cowboy, war hero, professional, patriot, self-mocking lover, "Greek hero," and old man. Good general analysis of essential ingredients in Wayne's career and acting can be found in Jeanne Basinger's "John Wayne: An Appreciation" and G. Hill's "John Wayne," while R. A. Higgins nicely summarizes his reputation and myth in his obituary, "John Wayne (1907–1979)." Eric Bentley, in "The Political Theater of John Wayne," calls Wayne the "most important American of our time" because he embodies dangerous political attitudes. Bentley gives a provocative, if undeveloped, argument for Wayne's influence in American society. The most thorough and insightful analyses of Wayne's meaning as a film actor and a cultural icon are "A Reappraisal of John Wayne" by Gary Edgerton and "People We Like: The Duke of Deception" by Terry Curtis Fox.

## Miscellaneous Print Sources

A variety of other sources related to Wayne and his career have appeared in print. The promotion campaign for *The Alamo* was extensive, producing *The Alamo: A Book on the Film by John Wayne* (1960) and *The Alamo* (1960) by Russell Birdwell, publicist for Wayne and United Artists. Also, the July 4, 1960, issue of *Life* magazine contains a major advertising section for the film.

Wayne inspired scattered literary efforts. Stefani B. Hinman's book, *The Malibu Million $ Rock* (1979), provides an account of the sculpting by Brett-Livingston Strong of a huge bust of Wayne from a boulder that fell from a cliff onto the highway at Malibu Beach. *The Canters of Thomas Parkinson, Chiefly Concerning John Wayne and His Horse and Many Incredulities* (1978) by Parkinson is an "epic" poem in five "canters." The poem's title speaks for itself. Another poem by Louis Phillips, "A Poem: Considering the Death of John Wayne," (1979) is a more standard tribute.

A number of comic books feature Wayne. A series of thirty-one issues of *John Wayne Adventure Comics* appeared between 1949 and 1955, and several of his films are part of a Dell series of "Movie Classics" comics published in the 1960's. Wayne also appeared as a character in single issues of *Big Tex* (1953), *Tim McCoy* (1948—an adaptation of the film *Red River*), *With the Marines on the Battlefronts of the World* (1953), and in a mail-order promotion series from Oxydol-Dreft (1950). Tom Tierney created *John Wayne Paper Dolls* (1981), with two Wayne figures in familiar stances and authentic paper costumes from thirty-one Wayne films.

Others in this miscellany are *Celebrity Homes II*, edited by
Paige Rense (1981), in which Wayne's home is presented; the
records of the House of Representatives' committee hearings
(1979) testimony in support of awarding a Congressional Medal
to Wayne; *The Big Trail*, a newsletter for Wayne enthusiasts edited
by Tim Lilley; and *America, Why I Love Her* by Wayne himself,
a paperback version of his RCA record of the same title.

## NOTE

1. In November 1991, a memoir of Wayne was published by his
daughter. Wayne, Aissa. *John Wayne, My Father*. New York: Ran-
dom House, 1991.

# 5

# INFORMATION SOURCES

## CHECKLIST OF WORKS CITED

### Books

*Biographies and Books about Wayne*

Barbour, Alan G. *John Wayne*. New York: Pyramid, 1974.
Bishop, George. *John Wayne: The Actor/The Man*. Ottawa, Illinois and Thornwood, New York: Caroline, 1979.
Boswell, John, and Jay David. *Duke: The John Wayne Album*. New York: Ballantine, 1979.
Carpozi, George, Jr. *The John Wayne Story*. New Rochelle: Arlington, 1972. Rev. ed. 1979.
Ferrari, Philippe J.-P. *John Wayne*. Solar, 1980.
Goldstein, Norm, for the Associated Press. *John Wayne: A Tribute*. New York: Holt, 1979.
*John Wayne*. E-Go Collectors Series 4. Sherman Oaks, California: E-Go Enterprises, 1976.
Kiesat, Charles John. *The Official John Wayne Reference Book*. Secaucus: Citadel, 1985.
*The Life and Times of John Wayne*. London: Hamlyn, 1979.
Pfeiffer, Lee. *The John Wayne Scrapbook*. Secaucus: Citadel, 1989.
Ramer, Jean. *Duke: The Real Story of John Wayne*. Grosset & Dunlap, 1973. Rev. ed. 1979.

Tomkies, Mike. *Duke: The Story of John Wayne*. Chicago: Regnery, 1971.

Shaw, Sam. *John Wayne in the Camera Eye*. New York: Peebles, 1979.

Shepherd, Donald, and Robert Slatzer, with Dave Grayson. *Duke: The Life and Times of John Wayne*. Garden City: Doubleday, 1985.

Stacy, Pat, with Beverly Linet. *Duke: A Love Story. An Intimate Memoir of John Wayne's Last Years*. New York: Atheneum, 1983.

Wayne, Pilar, with Alex Thorleifson. *John Wayne: My Life with the Duke*. New York: McGraw-Hill, 1987.

Whittingham, Richard (pseudo. David Paige). *John Wayne*. Mankato, Minnesota: Creative Children's Press, 1977.

Zolotow, Maurice. *Shooting Star: A Biography of John Wayne*. New York: Simon and Schuster, 1974. Rev. ed. 1979.

### Filmographies

Eyles, Allen. *John Wayne* (Original title: *John Wayne and the Movies*). New York: A. S. Barnes, 1976. Rev. ed. 1979.

Fernett, Gene. *Starring John Wayne*. Cocoa Beach: Cinememories, 1969.

Pascal, Francois, avec Francois Guerif et Pascal Merigeau. *John Wayne: Le Dernier Géant*. Editions Du Grand Bouchet, 1980.

Ricci, Mark, Boris Zmijewsky and Steve Zmijewsky. *The Films of John Wayne*. Secaucus: Citadel, 1970. Rev. ed. 1979.

### Books about Stars

Barbour, Alan G. *A Thousand and One Delights*. New York: MacMillan, 1971.

Castell, David. *Superstars of the 1970's*. London: B. C. Williams, 1974.

Corneau, Ernest N. *The Hall of Fame of Western Stars*. North Quincy, Massachusetts: Christopher, 1969.

Dyer, Richard. *Stars*. London: BFI, 1979.

Fernett, Gene. *Next Time Drive Off the Cliff!*. Cocoa Beach, Florida: Cinememories, n.d.

———. *Poverty Row*. Satellite Beach, Florida: Coral Reef Publications, 1973.

Finch, Christopher, and Linda Rosenkrantz. *Gone Hollywood*. Garden City, New York: Doubleday, 1979.

Goodman, Ezra. *The Fifty-Year Decline and Fall of Hollywood*. New York: Simon and Schuster, 1961.

Griffith, Richard. *The Movie Stars*. New York: Doubleday, 1970.

Hamblett, Charles. *The Hollywood Cage*. New York: Hart, 1966, 1969.

Hirsch, Phil. *Hollywood Uncensored*. New York: Pyramid, 1965.

Hopper, Hedda, and James Brough. *The Whole Truth and Nothing But*. Garden City: Doubleday, 1963.

Hyams, Joe. *Mislaid in Hollywood*. New York: P. H. Wyden, 1973.

Kobal, John. *Fifty Super-Stars*. New York: Bounty, 1974.

Miller, Lee O. *The Great Cowboy Stars of Movies and Westerns*. New York: Arlington House, 1979.

Morin, Edgar. *The Stars*. Paris: Seuil, 1957. Repr. trans. Richard Howard. New York: Grove, 1960.

Parish, James Robert. *Great Movie Heroes*. New York: Harper and Row, 1975.

Peary, Danny, ed. *Close-ups: The Movie Star Book*. New York: Workman, 1978.

Rivkin, Allen, and Laura Kerr. *Hello, Hollywood!* Garden City: Doubleday, 1962.

Schickel, Richard, and Allen Hurlburt. *The Stars: Personalities Who Made the Movies*. New York: Dial, 1962.

Walker, Alexander. *Stardom: The Hollywood Phenomenon*. New York: Stein and Day, 1970.

Weis, Elisabeth, ed. *The National Society of Film Critics on the Movie Star*. New York: Penguin, 1981.

Wilkie, Jane. *Confessions of an Ex-Fan Magazine Writer*. Garden City: Doubleday, 1981.

### Biographies of Others

Bogdanovich, Peter. *Allen Dwan: The Last Pioneer*. New York: Praeger, 1971.

Canutt, Yakima, with Oliver Drake. *Stunt Man*. New York: Walker and Company, 1979.

Capra, Frank. *The Name Above the Title: An Autobiography*. New York: MacMillan, 1971.

Ford, Dan. *Pappy: The Life of John Ford.* Englewood Cliffs, New Jersey: Prentice-Hall, 1979.

Garnett, Tay, with Fredda D. Balling. *Light Your Torches and Pull Up Your Tights.* New Rochelle: Arlington House, 1973.

Huston, John. *An Open Book.* New York: Alfred A. Knopf, 1980.

Madsen, Axel. *John Huston.* Garden City: Doubleday, 1978.

Roberson, "Bad Chuck," with Bodie Thoene. *The Fall Guy: 30 Years as the Duke's Double.* Canada: Hancock House, 1980.

Shavelson, Melville. *How to Make A Jewish Movie.* New York: W. H. Allen, 1971.

Sinclair, Andrew. *John Ford.* New York: Dial, 1979.

Stack, Robert. *Straight Shooting.* New York: MacMillan, 1980.

Wallis, Hal, and Charles Higham. *Starmaker: the Autobiography of Hal Wallis.* New York: MacMillan, 1980.

Walsh, Raoul. *Each Man in His Time: The Life Story of a Director.* New York: Farrar, Straus, and Giroux, 1974.

Wellman, William A. *A Short Time for Insanity.* New York: Hawthorne, 1974.

## Critical Studies

Anderson, Lindsay. *About John Ford.* New York: Plexus, 1981.

Anobile, Richard J., ed. *John Ford's Stagecoach Starring John Wayne.* New York Darien, 1975.

Barbour, Alan G. *John Wayne.* New York: Pyramid, 1974.

———. *The Thrill of It All.* New York: MacMillan, 1971.

Baxter, John. *The Cinema of John Ford.* New York: A. S. Barnes, 1971.

Belton, John. *The Hollywood Professionals: Howard Hawks, Frank Borzage, Edgar G. Ulmer.* New York: A. S. Barnes, 1974.

Blumenberg, Hans C. *Die Kamera in Augenhohe: Begegnungen Mit Howard Hawks.* Germany: Dumont, Buchverlag Koen, 1979.

Bogdanovich, Peter. *The Cinema of Howard Hawks.* New York: MOMA, 1962.

———. *John Ford.* Berkeley and Los Angeles: University of California P., 1967. Rev. ed. 1978.

———. *Pieces of Time.* New York: Dell, 1973.

Braudy, Leo. *The World in a Frame: What We See in Films.* Garden City: Anchor/Doubleday, 1976.

Brown, Peter H. *The Real Oscar: The Story Behind the Academy Awards.* Westport, Connecticut: Arlington House, 1981.

Brownlow, Kevin. *The War, the West and the Wilderness.* New York: Alfred A. Knopf, 1979.

Burrows, Michael. *John Ford and Andrew V. McLaglen.* Cornwall: Primestyle, 1970.

Calder, Jenni. *There Must Be a Lone Ranger: The American West in Film and in Reality.* New York: Taplinger, 1974.

Canham, Kingsley. *The Hollywood Professionals: Michael Curtiz, Raoul Walsh, Henry Hathaway.* New York: A. S. Barnes, 1973.

Clapham, Walter. *Western Movies.* London: Octopus Books, 1974.

Fenin, George N., and William K. Everson. *The Western: From Silents to the Seventies.* New York: Penguin, 1973.

French, Philip. *Westerns: Aspects of a Movie Genre.* New York: Oxford UP, 1973. Rev. ed. 1977.

Froug, William. *The Screenwriter Looks at the Screenwriter.* New York: MacMillan, 1972.

Haskell, Molly. *From Reverence to Rape: The Treatment of Women in the Movies.* New York: Holt, 1974, 1987.

Hine, Robert V. *The American West: An Interpretative History.* Boston: Little, Brown, 1973.

Kagan, Norman. *The War Film.* New York: Jove, 1974.

Kaminsky, Stuart M. *American Film Genres: Approaches to a Critical Theory of Popular Film.* New York: Pflaum, 1974.

Lenihan, John H. *Showdown: Confronting America in the Western Film.* Urbana: U of Illinois P, 1980.

Levy, Emanuel. *John Wayne: Prophet of the American Way of Life.* Metuchen, New Jersey: Scarecrow, 1988.

Luhr, William, and Peter Lehman. *Authorship and Narrative in the Cinema.* New York: Putnam's, 1977.

Malone, Michael. *Heroes of Eros: Male Sexuality in the Movies.* New York: E. P. Dutton, 1979.

Maltby, Richard. *Harmless Entertainment: Hollywood and the Ideology of Consensus.* Metuchen, New Jersey: Scarecrow, 1983.

McBride, Joseph, ed. *Focus on Howard Hawks.* Englewood Cliffs, New Jersey: Prentice-Hall, 1972.

McBride, Joseph, and Michael Wilmington. *John Ford.* New York: DaCapo, 1975.

McConnell, Frank. *Storytelling and Mythmaking: Images from Film and Literature.* New York: Oxford UP, 1979.

McDonald, Archie P. *Shooting Stars: Heroes and Heroines of Western Film*. Bloomington: Indiana UP, 1987.

McGhee, Richard D. *John Wayne: Actor, Artist, Hero*. New York: McFarland, 1990.

Mellen, Joan. *Big Bad Wolves: Masculinity in the American Film*. New York: Pantheon, 1977.

Meyer, William. *The Making of the Great Westerns*. New Rochelle: Arlington House, 1979.

Nachbar, Jack, ed. *Focus on the Western*. Englewood Cliffs, New Jersey: Prentice-Hall, 1974.

Nichols, Dudley. *Stagecoach* (from the story by Ernest Haycox) in *Twenty Best Film Plays*. John Gassner and Dudley Nichols, eds. New York: Crown, 1943. (Edition with Haycox story. Nicola Hayden, ed. New York: Simon and Schuster, 1971.)

Pechter, William S. *Twenty-Four Times a Second*. New York: Harper and Row, 1970.

Place, J. A. *The Non-Western Films of John Ford*. Secaucus, New Jersey: Citadel, 1979.

———. *The Western Films of John Ford*. Secaucus, New Jersey: Citadel, 1974.

Rieupeyrout, Jean-Louis. *La Grande Aventure du Western: Du Far West a Hollywood*. Paris: Les Editions du Cerf, 1964.

Savage, William W., Jr. *The Cowboy Hero: His Image in American History and Culture*. Norman: U of Oklahoma P, 1979.

Schatz, Thomas. *Hollywood Genres: Formulas, Filmmaking and the Studio System*. Philadelphia: Temple UP, 1981.

Schickel, Richard. *The Men Who Made Movies*. New York: Atheneum, 1975.

Silver, Charles. *The Western Film*. New York: Pyramid, 1976.

Smith, Julian. *Looking Away: Hollywood and Vietnam*. New York: Scribner's, 1975.

Solomon, Stanley J. *Beyond Formula: American Film Genres*. New York: Harcourt Brace, 1976.

Spoto, Donald. *Camerado: Hollywood and the American Man*. New York: NAL, 1978.

Suid, Lawrence. *Guts and Glory: Great American War Movies*. Reading, Massachusetts: Addison-Wesley, 1978.

Thomas, Bob, ed. *Directors in ACTION*. Indianapolis: Bobbs-Merrill, 1973.

Tuska, Jon. *The Filming of the West*. Garden City: Doubleday, 1976.
———. *The Vanishing Legion: A History of Mascot Pictures, 1927–1935*. Jefferson, North Carolina: 1981.
Warman, Eric, and Tom Vallance, eds. *Westerns: A Preview Special*. London: Golden Pleasure, 1964.
Willis, Donald C. *The Films of Howard Hawks*. Metuchen, New Jersey: Scarecrow, 1975.
Wood, Michael. *America in the Movies or "Santa Maria, It Had Slipped My Mind."* New York: Dell, 1975.

**Articles**

*Interview Articles*

Bogdanovich, Peter. "Duke's Gone West." *New York* 25 June 1979: 67–70.
Eyman, Scott. "Looking Back: John Wayne Talking to Scott Eyman." *Focus on Film* 20 (Spring 1975): 17–23.
Flatley, George. "Cowboy or Cop; Wayne Never Wanes." *New York Times Magazine* 30 December 1973: 1.
Gaugin, Lorraine. "Duke in Durango." *National Review* 27 April 1973: 472–3.
Haskell, Molly. "What Makes John Wayne Larger Than Life." *The Village Voice* 16 August 1976: 69–70.
——— "Wayne, Westerns, and Women." *Ladies Home Journal* July 1976: 76–7, 88–94.
Litchtenstein, Roy. "Hey Mister! Wayne Marks First 50 Years." *New York Times Magazine* 27 January 1976: 29.
Macklin, F. A. " 'I Come Ready': An Interview with John Wayne." *Film Heritage* 19 (Summer 1975): 1–33.
Martin, Pete. "Ladies Like 'Em Rugged." *Saturday Evening Post* 2 December 1950: 19. Collected in *Pete Martin Calls On*. New York: Simon and Schuster, 1962. Also reprt. in *Saturday Evening Post* July 1978: 62.
McInerney, Joe. "John Wayne Talks Tough." *Film Comment* 8 (Sept-Oct 1972): 52–55.
Miller, Edwin. "Do You Ever Think of Duke as Big Daddy?" *Seventeen* October 1971: 122–3, 178, 182.

Morgan, Thomas B. "God and Man in Hollywood." *Esquire* May
    1963: 74+. Reprt. in *Self-Creations: Thirteen Impersonalit-
    ies*. New York: Holt, 1965.
Playboy editors. "Playboy Interview: John Wayne." *Playboy* 18 (May
    1971): 75-92. Included in this book.
Ronan, M. "Two Screen Cowboys Talk About the Reel and Real
    West." *Senior Scholastic* 6 December 1971: 10-11.
Sutton, D. "John Wayne: Image vs. Man." *Saturday Evening Post*
    March 1976: 54-74.

*Articles in Film Journals*

Albert, Stephen. "*The Shootist*: redemption of discredited authority."
    *Jump Cut* 26 (Dec 1981): 9-12.
"Alternate Titles to John Wayne Films." *Classic Films Collection*
    (Fall 1976): 41.
Andrade, Valerio. "O Ultimo Cowboy." *Filme Cultura* 8 (March
    1974): 19-22.
Applebaum, Ralph. "Making 'The Shootist': an interview with Don
    Siegel." *Filmmakers Newsletter* 9 (Oct 1976): 28-32.
Basinger, Jeanne. "John Wayne: An Appreciation." *American Film* 1
    (June 1976): 50, 52-53.
Beaver, Jim. "John Wayne." *Films in Review* 28 (May 1977): 265-84.
    Letters in Aug-Sept 1977 and Feb 1978 issues provide correc-
    tions and additions.
Belton, John. "John Wayne: As Sure as the Turning o' the Earth."
    *Velvet Light Trap* 7 (Winter 1972-73): 25-28.
Bendtsen, T. "Beloved Husband and Father." *Chaplin* 22:6 (1971):
    253-62.
Bentley, Eric. "The Political Theater of John Wayne." *Film Society
    Review* 7 (March-May 1972): 51-60.
Bernstein, Barbara. "Not Likely." *Focus!* Spring 1970: 3-7.
Bernstein, Judith. "The Valley of the Shadow." *Focus!* Autumn 1972:
    13-18.
Bidault, Anne-Marie. "John Wayne et ses Mythologies: Un Grand
    Géant au Beret Vert." *Cinema* July-Aug 1979: 80-91.
Brode, Douglas. "Reflections on the Tradition of the Movie West-
    ern." *Cineaste* 2 (Fall 1968): 2-6.

Budd, Michael. "Genre, Director and Stars in John Ford's Westerns: Fonda, Wayne, Stewart and Widmark." *Wide Angle* 2 (1978): 52–61.

Buhler, W.-E. "John Wayne." *Filmkritik* 16 (Jan 1972): 42–46.

Card, James V. D. *"The Searchers:* by Alan LeMay and by John Ford." *Literature and Film Quarterly* 16:1 (Jan 1988): 2–9.

"Comments on John Wayne." *Film Heritage* 10 (Summer 1975): 34–38.

Crawley, Tony. "Action Speaks Louder Than Dialogue." *Cinema* 1979: 122–127.

D'Arcy, Susan. "The Indestructibles." *Films Illustrated* 5 (Nov 1975): 92–3.

" 'Do I Get to Play the Drunk This Time?' " *Sight and Sound* 40 (Spring 1971): 97–100.

Edgerton, Gary. "A Reappraisal of John Wayne." *Films in Review* May 1986: 282–289.

Fox, Terry Curtis. "People We Like: The Duke of Deception." *Film Comment* 15 (Sept-Oct 1979): 68–70.

Gray, Martin. "No-Contract Star." *Films and Filming* 3 (March 1957): 15.

Hall, Dennis. "Tall in the Saddle." *Films and Filming* 16 (Oct 1969): 12–22.

Higgins, R. A. "John Wayne (1907-1979)." *Cineaste* 9 (Fall 1979): 60.

Hill, G. "John Wayne." *Kinema* 3 (Autumn 1971): 5–12.

Hoch, Winston. "The Vietnam War as Filmed for *The Green Berets.*" *American Cinematographer* 49 (Sept 1968): 654–57.

Jameson, Richard T. "Talking and Doing in *Rio Bravo.*" *Velvet Light Trap* 12 (Spring 1974): 26–30.

Kaminsky, Stuart. "Legend of the Lost." *Velvet Light Trap* 14 (Winter 1975): 25–29.

Kitses, Jim. "The Rise and Fall of the American West: Borden Chase Interviewed." *Film Comment* 6 (Winter 1970-71): 14–21.

Lightman, Herb A. "Filming *The Alamo* in Todd AO." *American Cinematographer* 41 (Nov 1960): 662–663.

Mace, J. W. "John Wayne Rareties." *Classic Films Collection* 38 (April 1973): 30–31.

Mariani, J. "John Wayne's Women." *Millimeter* 4 (July-Aug 1976): 50–53, 67.

McBride, Joseph, and Gerald Peary. "Hawks Talks: New Anecdotes from the Old Master." *Film Comment* 10 (May-June 1974): 44-52.

McGhee, Richard D. "John Wayne: Hero with a Thousand Faces." *Literature/Film Quarterly* 16:1 (Jan 1988): 10-21.

Ockersen, T. " 'Ik ben net een hoer dies geen geld kan weest ann': interview met Don Siegel." *Skoop* 12 (October 1976): 6-8.

Sarris, Andrew. "Cactus Rosebud or the Man Who Shot Liberty Valance." *Film Culture* 25 (Summer 1962): 13-15.

Sinclair, Andrew. "Man on Horseback: The Seven Faces of John Wayne." *Sight and Sound* 48 (Autumn 1979): 232-5.

Sklar, Robert. "Empire to the West: *Red River.*" *Cineaste* 9 (Fall 1978): 3-17. Reprt. in *American History/American Film*. John E. O'Connor and Martin A. Jackson, eds. New York: Frederick Ungar, 1979. 168-81.

Suid, Lawrence. "Hollywood and Vietnam." *Film Comment* 15 (Sept-Oct 1979): 20-25.

———. "The Making of the Green Berets." *Journal of Popular Film* 6:2 (1977): 106-125.

Thiede, Karl. "John Wayne: A Comprehensive Filmography." *Views and Reviews* 1 (Fall 1969): 36-40. Letters in subsequent issues provide additions.

Wayne, John. "Why I Turned Producer and Director." *Journal of Screen Producers Guild* Sept 1960: 23-24.

## Miscellaneous Print Sources

*The Alamo: A Book by John Wayne.* California: Deny Morrison et al, 1960.

*Big Tex.* Toby Press, 1953. Comics, issue 1.

Birdwell, Russell. *The Alamo.* United Artists, 1960.

Dell "Movie Classics" comics series, 1960s.

Hinman, Stefani. *The Malibu Million $ Rock.* Santa Monica: Dennis-Landman, 1979.

*John Wayne Adventure Comics.* Toby Press, 1949-53. Comics, issues 1-31.

*Life.* 4 July 1960, promotional insert.

Lilley, Tim, ed. *The Big Trail* (newsletter). 540 Stanton Avenue, Akron, Ohio 44301.

Oxydol-Dreft comics series, 1950. Issue 4.

Parkinson, Thomas F. *The Canters of Thomas Parkinson, Chiefly Concerning John Wayne and His Horse and Many Incredulities*. Berkeley, California: Thorp Springs Press, 1978.

Phillips, Louis. "A Poem: Considering the Death of John Wayne." *Journal of Popular Film and Television* 7:3 (1979): 265.

Rense, Paige, ed. (for *Architecture Digest*). *Celebrity Homes II*. Louisiana: Knapp, 1981.

Tierney, Tom. *John Wayne Paper Dolls*. New York: Dover, 1981.

*Tim McCoy*. Charlton, 1948. Comics, issue 16.

United States Congress. House Committee on Banking, Finance, and Urban Affairs. Hearing HR 3767, 21 May 1979. 96th Congress, 1st session. Washington, DC: GPO, 1979.

Wayne, John. *America, Why I Love Her*. New York: Ballantine, 1979.

*With the Marines on the Battlefronts of the World*. Toby Press, 1953. Comics, issue 1.

## ADDITIONAL PRINT SOURCES

### Popular Magazine Articles

Because there are many magazine articles, and most have self-explanatory titles, I list them here without comment.

Alexander, T. "Great Fox Powell, John Wayne, Magic-Dirt Medicine Show." *Fortune* 27 March 1978: 46–66+.

Ardmore, J. "Cancer Doesn't Fight Fair." *Family Health* Sept 1976: 30–33.

*Arizona Highways*. Special issue of "Movies in Arizona." Sept 1981: see especially William R. Florence, "John Ford . . . the Duke . . . and Monument Valley," 22–31, 34–37.

Bacon, James. "John Wayne, the Last Cowboy." *Us* 27 June 1978: 23–25.

Barron, F. "Duke Takes Harvard." *Progressive* March 1974: 51.

Barthel, J. "John Wayne, Superhawk." *New York Times Magazine* 24 Dec 1967: 4. Reply with rejoinder, 1 Jan 1967: 4.

Bell, J. N. "John Wayne's Scrapbook." *Good Housekeeping* June 1976: 116–119+.

"Big John." *Newsweek* 1 March 1965: 86.

Bogdanovich, Peter. "Hollywood." *Esquire* May 1972: 66.

Byron, Stuart. " 'The Searchers': Cult Movie of the New Hollywood." *New York* 5 March 1979: 45-58.

Cavinder, Fred. "A Congressional Medal for Duke." *Saturday Evening Post* Sept 1979: 31.

───── "John Wayne: Everybody's Hero." *Saturday Evening Post* Sept 1979: 36-37.

───── "John Wayne: How He Won the West." *Saturday Evening Post* July 1979: 58-64.

───── "John Wayne's Other Roles." *Saturday Evening Post* Oct 1979: 32-35.

"Celebrity Visit with: John Wayne." *Good Housekeeping* May 1978: 140-3.

Corliss, Richard. "Kitsch Kitsch Bang Bang." *New Times* 3 Sept 1976: 60.

Cousins, Norman. "In Praise of Famous Men." *Saturday Review* 1 Sept 1979: 8.

Deedy, J. "News and Views: Government Hand in Production of *The Green Berets*" *Commonweal* 28 June 1968: 426.

Didion, Joan. "John Wayne: A Love Song." *Saturday Evening Post* 14 August 1965: 76-79.

"Duke and Sister Kate, Too." *Time* 18 Nov 1974: 133.

"Duke at 60." *Time* 9 June 1967: 67.

"Duke's Disk." *Newsweek* 19 March 1973: 85.

"The Duke is Back: On the Job Again." *TV Guide* 23 Sept 1978: 10.

"East and West Meet in Wayne." *Life* 7 May 1956: 161.

"Editor's Note" (letter from John Wayne). *Saturday Evening Post* July 1979: 4-5.

Eels, G. "Ed Sullivan's Changing Show." *Look* 16 Feb 1960: 67.

Eyman, Scott. "Film Clips: the Death of a Giant, the Birth of a Legend." *Ohio Magazine* August 1979: 66.

Fowler, G. "The Meaning of an American Man: John Wayne at 70." *Human Events* 28 May 1977: 8.

Friedman, B. J. "Could Dirty Harry Take Rooster Cogburn?" *Esquire* Sept 1976: 10.

"Frontlines: Balancing His Act." *Mother Jones* May 1978: 9.

"Garbo, Dietrich, Cooper and Wayne: all were caught on film by the legendary Cecil Beaton." *People* 29 Oct 1980: 125-6.

Gault, J. "Metaphor for His Time." *Macleans* 25 June 1979: 26-7.

Goodman, M. "Full Ahead, Mr. Wayne." *Motor Boating and Sailing* Nov 1978: 58-61.

Grenier, Richard. "John Wayne's Image." *Commentary* Sept 1979: 79–81.

Hamilton, J. "John Wayne." *Look* 2 August 1960: 83.

Hano, J. "John Wayne: A Man in Every Sense of the Word." *Good Housekeeping* Oct 1965: 83.

Hart, Jeffrey. "John Wayne—1907–1979: The Legend Will Linger." *Human Events* 23 June 1979: 16.

Hendrickson, P. J. "John Wayne: The Iron Duke; with Report by Joan Didion." *Saturday Evening Post* Spring 1972: 84–91.

Hepburn, Katherine. "Hooked on John Wayne." *TV Guide* 17 Sept 1977: 63.

Itria, H. "Big John." *Look* 11 August 1953: 67.

Jackovich, K. G., and M. Sennet. "Children of John Wayne, Susan Hayward and Dick Powell fear that fallout killed their parents." *People* 10 Nov 1980: 4–7.

Jennings, Dean. "Woes of a Box Office King: John Wayne." *Saturday Evening Post* 27 Oct 1980: 28.

"John Wayne as the Last Hero." *Time* 8 August 1969: 54.

"John Wayne, Man of Courage." *Saturday Evening Post* July/August 1979: 68.

"John Wayne Rides Again." *Life* May 1965: 69.

"John Wayne's America." *Good Housekeeping* Nov 1977: 138–41.

"John Wayne's Green Beret." *Nation* 11 Dec 1967: 614.

Johnson, G. "John Ford: Maker of Hollywood Stars." *Coronet* Dec 1953: 133–40.

"Kate and the Duke Team Up to Make Hollywood History." *People* 18 Nov 1974: 8.

Kaufmann, Stanley. "Wayning." *New Republic* 11 Sept 1976: 24–5.

Kluge, P. F. "First and Last, A Cowboy." *Life* 28 Jan 1972: 42–6.

Kroll, Jack. "John Wayne, End as a Man." *Newsweek* 25 June 1979: 76–79.

Leider, R. A. "John Wayne: Supercop." *Show* Nov 1973: 46–9.

Liston, J. "At Home with John Wayne." *American Home* April 1961: 13.

Marshall, P. "Mini-Holiday." *Holiday* June 1975: 76.

McGuire, Jerry. "The Bronze Duke." *Saturday Evening Post* Sept 1979: 42–44.

Morris, George. "The Duke and Me." *Texas Monthly* August 1979: 123.

Nugent, J. P. "John Wayne's Ordeal." *Newsweek* 25 July 1960: 107.

Page, W. "Man's Man." *Field and Stream* Jan 1966: 30.

Reagan, Ronald. "Unforgettable John Wayne." *Reader's Digest* Oct 1979: 114–19.

Reddy, J. "John Wayne Rides Again and Again and Again." *Reader's Digest* Sept 1970: 138–42.

Richter, W. D. "Hellfire Made to Order." *Popular Science* Dec 1968: 48.

Riley, C. "John Wayne Dethroned." *Ebony* Sept 1962: 127–8.

Saal, H. "John Wayne's Hit Record." *Newsweek* 19 March 1973: 85A.

Sarris, Andrew. "John Wayne's Strange Legacy." *New Republic* 4 August 1979: 33–36.

Schickel, Richard. "Duke: Images from a Lifetime." *Time* 25 June 1979: 50–51.

Scott, V., ed. "John Wayne: His Wife Explains the Man Behind the Legend." *Ladies Home Journal* Nov 1971: 72.

Shapon, R. L. "United We Fall; Divided We Stand." *Saturday Review* 2 Jan 1971: 59.

Simon, John. "Wayne Damage." *New York* 30 August 1976: 50–52.

Stone, M. "Hero to Fit the Image." *U.S. News and World Report* 28 May 1979: 80.

"Stronger Sex Makes Strong Box Office." *Life* 31 May 1954: 93–96.

Sutton, D. "John Wayne is 'McQ'!" *Motor Trend* March 1974: 54.

Scott, M. "John Wayne." *Cosmopolitan* Nov 1954: 26.

Thomas, Bob. "John Wayne: The Last American Hero." *Look* 16 April 1979: 34–37.

"Wages of Virtue." *Time* 3 March 1952: 64.

Wayne, John. "Good Times: Duke on America." *Saturday Evening Post* Sept 1979: 38, 40.

Whitney, Dwight. "TV Update: ABC-CBS Shoot-out Developing Over Wayne Biography." *TV Guide* 18 August 1979: A3.

Zolotow, Maurice. "How the Duke Made Friends with Death." *Los Angeles* March 1979: 152.

——— "John Wayne: What Makes Him an American Institution." *50 Plus* Oct 1978: 12–17.

## Fan Magazine Articles

Fan magazines are an invaluable source for charting the development of a star's career and image. Unfortunately, they have not been systematically collected or indexed. Isolated collections exist and can be traced through union catalogues. Only *Photoplay* has been indexed. The following list is my indexing (including *Photoplay*) of articles about John Wayne up to the time of his death in fan magazine holdings of the Library of Congress. I group articles by magazine, listing them in chronological order. The LOC holdings have gaps, and I have indicated these.

### *Hollywood* (volumes 23–32, 1934–March 1943)

Franchey, John. "Life with Father." August 1942: 26, 55.
Wayne, John. "My Favorite Recipe." January 1943: 20.

### *Modern Screen* (1931–1962, 1967–June 1977; 1976 incomplete)

Baskette, Kirtley. "Gentlemen Johnny." February 1943: 46–47, 110–113.
MacNeil, Morgan. "John Wayne's Double Life," August 1949: 36–37, 99–100.
Carlile, Tom. "Wonderful Lug." August 1950: 30–31, 71, 73.
Carlile, Tom. "Look Out for This Guy." August 1951: 54–55, 64.
Baskette, Kirtley. "Top Man." January 1952: 20–21, 77–79.
Henaghan, Jim. "I Love You, Chata." April 1952: 40–41, 103–105.
Henaghan, Jim. "Second Honeymoon." June 1952: 30–31, 81–82.
Saunders, Marsha. "The On Again, Off Again Waynes." September 1952: 58–59, 64–65.
Dexter, Richard. "It Had to Happen." November 1952: 28, 68.
Henaghan, Jim. "Man on the Move." April 1953: 39–40, 107–108.
Charles, Arthur L. "Has John Wayne Gone Again?" June 1953: 16, 33–35.
Cummings, Sandy. "The Battling Waynes in Court." August 1953: 24, 95–96.
Cummings, Sandy. "The Big Guy Takes the Stand." November 1953: 14, 76–77.
Collins, Imogene. "Behind Closed Doors." February 1954: 36–37, 66–69.
Collins, Imogene. "Why Duke Likes Them Latin." June 1954: 38–39, 85–86.
Henaghan, Jim. "The Big Man Comes Home." October 1954: 44–45, 96–99.

Wade, Jack. "The Duke Goes West." January 1955: 36–37, 68–69.

Wayne, Pilar. "When We're Alone." July 1956: 36–37, 76–77.

"John Wayne's Children Tell All." September 1956: 66–67, 87.

Wayne, John. "Here's My Reply." October 1956: 63, 89–90.

Henaghan, Jim. "Should I Be an Actor or a Priest?" November 1956: 44–45, 87–89.

Wayne letter to wife. June 1957: 54–55.

Banning, Don. "Three Minutes in the Fires of Hell." April 1958: 21, 75–76.

"Did John Wayne Risk His Wife and Child's Lives?" August 1959: 28, 74.

Tusher, William. "His Second Ordeal with Tragedy." September 1967: 46, 63–64.

Waterbury, Ruth. "How Four Generations of Waynes Spend Christmas Together." January 1969: 28, 60–62.

Kharisma, Petina. "Is He Now Too Old For His Wife?" September 1969: 38, 86–87.

"Visit His Small World." November 1969: 40–53.

Man, May. " 'God You Have Been More Than Good To Me and Mine . . . .' " May 1970: 42–43, 62–66.

Gregory, James. "John Wayne—the Crazy Things He Does! His Wife's Own Story." September 1970: 38–39, 42–45, 28–30, 89–90.

Fletcher, Adele. "Cancer Claims His Brother." November 1970: 54–55, 68–76.

Gregory, James. "Viet Cong Flag Waver Tries to Jail Him!" December 1971: 48–49, 55, 4.

del Lobo, Susannah. "Talks About His Private Life With His Teenage Daughter." May 1972: 34–35, 68, 70.

Carpozi, George, Jr. "Exclusive Interview with Pilar: 'We've Been Married in the Eyes of the World—But He's Never Home.' " March 1974: 48–49, 66–70.

"Wayne With Hepburn in *Rooster Cogburn*: Behind the Scenes Rumors of Romance and Illness." December 1975: 46–47, 64.

"John Wayne: The Duke's 50th Anniversary." June 1976: 60–64.

*Motion Picture* (volumes 1–65, February 1911–June 1976, 1966 incomplete)

Goldbeck, Elisabeth. "Samson of Hollywood: John Wayne Needed a Haircut and Became Famous." February 1931: 76, 112.

Hamilton, Sara. "Yip-ee: The Cowboy Rides Again." June 1936: 34-35, 72.

Whitehead, Hal. "Future Favorites—John Wayne." July 1937: 15.

Schratt, Gene. "Male Oomph." November 1940: 45, 72.

"John Wayne." June 1940: 32.

Cover of April 1944 with Paulette Goddard, from *Reap the Wild Wind*.

Martin, Denis. "Are They Happier Apart?" May 1944: 44-45.

Weller, Helen. "Made in Heaven: Let's Pretend You're Mrs. John Wayne." April 1950: 42-43, 75-77.

Maynard, John. "It Couldn't Happen to a Nicer Guy." September 1950: 34-35, 74-75.

Allen, Don. "It's Been Fun, But . . . ." June 1951: 36-37, 72-73.

Bond, Ward. "The Duke and I." September 1951: 48-49, 68-70.

Valdes, Marguerita. "Is a Romantic Legend Over?" May 1952: 48-49, 77-78.

Wayne, John. "I'm Two Different Guys." August 1952: 30-31, 76.

Wandworth, John. "From 'Prisoner' to Playboy." December 1952: 42-43, 73-74.

Mason, H. M., Jr. " 'I Hate Phonies.' " June 1953: 55, 73.

Maynard, John. "Duke Likes it Latin." August 1953: 28-29, 64.

Taylor, Ross. "Is John Wayne a Sucker?" September 1953: 6, 10.

Paul, Julie. "Rugged Lover." August 1954: 24-25, 55-56.

Tusher, Bill. "Wayne." December 1954: 44-47, 70-72.

Henaghan, Jim. "It Happened in Hawaii." February 1955: 28-29, 75-76.

Willoughby, Bob. "Duke Takes a Holiday." July 1955: 28-29.

Barbier and Hamilton. "John Wayne—Like Father, Like Son." February 1956: 44-45.

Henaghan, Jim. "Pat Wayne—Papa Loves Patrick." May 1956: 36-37.

"Secrets I've Never Confessed." July 1956: 26.

Wayne, John. "Hollywood's Most Tempting Women." July 1956: 48-51, 56.

"Duke Gains a Son." September 1956: 12-13.

Henaghan, Jim. "Duke—The Man Who'd Dare the Devil." November 1956: 24-25, 70-75.

Wayne, Pat. "I'm Glad My Dad's An Actor." August 1958: 56-57, 74-75.

Ardmore, Jane. "The Lustiest Man in Town." December 1962: 34, 70-72.

"Duke's Daughter Gets Married." July 1964: 54-55, 65.

"The Duke's Message to the King: 'You Can Beat It, Nat—I Did!' "
   March 1965: 43–45, 64–65.
"Are You Home to Stay, Daddy?" May 1965: 48–51, 60.
"John Wayne in Hospital!" November 1965: 28–29, 70–71.
"I Can't Afford to Die—We're Having Another Baby!" January 1966:
   17, 60–62.
"The Man Who'd Dare the Devil." March 1966: 36–37, 84–86.
"John Wayne's Beautiful Baby!" June 1966: 40–43.
"A Secret of Youth John Wayne and Cary Grant Can Teach Women."
   October 1966: 38–39, 72.
"Don't Let My Grandson Die." January 1966: 34–35, 81–82.
"Nobody's Shoving Me Off This Earth!" March 1968: 52–53, 91–92.
"The Real Truth About John Wayne—David Janssen Feud." April
   1968, 38–39, 57–59.
"I'll Continue . . . Till the Man Upstairs Knocks At My Door." June
   1969: 24–25, 72–73.
"The High Price John Wayne Pays for Love!" September 1969:
   20–21, 92–93.
"Why Friends are Shaking Their Heads About John Wayne and His
   Wife." February 1970: 58–59, 82–83.
"John Wayne Please Come Home!" March 1970: 44–45, 75–76.
"How Sammy Davis Kept the Mafia from Killing John Wayne" (2
   parts). June 1970: 42, 89; August 1970: 47, 74–75.
"John Wayne: A Tribute to the Duke." September 1970: 46–53.
Carpozi, George, Jr. "We Expose John Wayne's Fake Son." Novem-
   ber 1970: 24–25, 82–83.
Gregory, James. "Memories of a Beloved Brother He Lost." Novem-
   ber 1970: 22–23, 80.
"I Don't Even Know What a Generation Gap Is." October 1971:
   81–21, 88–89.
"There's No Generation Gap That Soap, Water, and Love Can't
   Cure." April 1973: 36–38, 54–56.
Tusher, Will. "I Can't Stand Politics." August 1976: 46–48, 50, 52.

*Movie Action Magazine* (volume 1, November
1935–June 1936)

"The New Frontier." December 1935: 26–38. (a "novelized" version,
   with stills, of one of Wayne's B westerns).
"Lawless Range." February 1936: 30–41.

"The Oregon Trail." March 1936: 112–122.

*Movie Fan* (volumes 1–10, Winter 1946–March
1955; then merged with *Screen Life*)

"John Wayne." September—October 1949: 28–29.
"John Wayne." March—April 1950: 20–21.
"Janet Leigh—John Wayne." January—February 1951: 26.
"John Wayne." May—June 1951: 36–37.
Latrobe, Rosa. "All Mixed Up and Everywhere to Go." December
1952: 46–48.
"Long Man—Short Sofa." July 1953: 36–37.
Arness, Jim. "I Know the Real Duke." September 1954: 46–47, 57.

*Movieland* (volumes 1–18, February 1943–May
1961; volumes 13–14 missing; changed to
*Movieland and TV Time* in volume 16)

Morgan, Fred. "Handsome Hunk of Sex Appeal." August 1949:
42–43, 70.
Wayne, John. "On the Level." May 1950: 30–31, 78–79.
"The Wayne Wallop." May 1951: 32–33.
"I'm a Wayne Fan, Too!" (a personal report by John's secretary to
Viola Moore). July 1951: 62–63, 74.
Wayne, John. "The Turning Point in My Life." October 1951: 46–47,
73.
Wayne, Toni. "My Heart Belongs to Daddy." April 1952: 24–25,
66–67.
"John Wayne's Fight to Save His Marriage." May 1952: 30–32.
"I Cannot Go On. . . . " November 1952: 17–18.
"That Old Wayne Magic." May 1953: 24–25.
"Why Women Love John Wayne." July 1953: 17–18.
Carlin, E. J. "Big John's Bit Switch." November 1953: 38–39, 74–
76.
"3-D Dynamite." January 1954: 20–21.
McClure, Spec. "Everybody . . . But Everybody . . . Loves John
Wayne." February 1954: 38–41, 79–81.
"People Who Make News: The Wary One—John Wayne." April
1954: 58.
"The Truth About Hollywood's Marriage-Shy Men." May 1954: 32.

"How Hollywood Lives." June 1954: 35.
Wayne, John. "Mistakes I've Made." June 1954: 48–49, 73–75.
"John's Current Love." November 1954: 58.
"I Lead a Double Life." March 1957: 50–51, 56, 58, 60.
Meade, Susan. "Why John Wayne Can't Forget." September 1956: 40, 68–69.
Quirk, Lawrence J. "Hollywood's Terrific Ten." June 1959: 50–51, 62–66.
"All Time Greats." 1961 Annual: 71.

*Movie Life* (volumes 1–40, November 1937–1977)

"Tropical Temptress." December 1940: 52–53.
"Republic Remembers." April 1941: 56.
"Location Hot or Cold." May 1941: 57.
"Allegheny Frontier." November 1939: 56.
"Around the Studios." December 1939: 58.
"Dark Command." April 1940: 56.
"Dark Command Has World Premier in Lawrence, Kansas." July 1940: 54–55.
"Long Voyage Home." September 1940: 60.
"Reap the Wild Wind." April 1942: 42–43.
"Stars of the Western Sky." May 1942: 56.
"30th Anniversary Party." June 1942: 24.
"No Holds Barred: Furious Fights from 'In Old California.' " August 1942: 62–63.
"Flying Tigers in Hollywood." September 1942: 58–59.
"In Old Oklahoma." December 1943: 50–51.
"First Seabees Film." April 1944: 12–13.
"Wayne in New Guinea." June 1944: 14.
"Around the Lots." January 1946: 80–81.
"Movie Life of John Wayne." July 1946: 29.
"Roughin It, Sorta." March 1948: 32–33, 107.
"Riding High." June 1949: 6.
"Going Legit." June 1949: 68–69.
"Leading the Parade." December 1949: 66–69.
"On Sunday Afternoon." August 1950: 43.
"Trail Blazers." August 1950: 80–83.
"The Duke and the Duchess." September 1950: 28–31.
"Those Terrific Torsos." November 1950: 42–8.

"Safety First." April 1951: 80.
"The Duke in London." April 1957: 82–83.
"Faraway Faces." August 1951: 68.
"10 Magnetic Males." April 1953: 29.
"The Winners." May 1953: 90.
"Everybody Talking About: John and Pilar." June 1953: 16.
"Life with Duke." September 1953: 60–61.
"John's Mexican Heartburn." May 1954: 21–23.
"Roughing It!" October 1954: 46–49.
"The Honeymooners." February 1955: 16.
"How Hollywood Makes Love: Violent." December 1955: 44.
"Great Expectations." January 1956: 10.
"John Wayne's Movie Life: The Adventure of A Nice Violent Guy."
          August 1956: 42–47.
"At Ease." November 1957: 68.
"We're Fighting Our Dads: Pat Wayne." November 1957: 32.
"Intimate Love Secrets: Pilar and John Wayne." January 1958: 39.
"Around the Lots." December 1961: 64.
"John Wayne: In the Golden Circle." April 1962: 8, 53.
Morris, Jane. "John Wayne: Man or Beast?" November 1962: 34–35,
          50.
"Flat-Broke Millionaire." January 1964: 40–46.
"Can Chakiris Save Wayne's Marriage?" March 1964: 24–25, 76–77.
"Dee, Wayne Nearly Killed." April 1964: 12.
"John Wayne Needs Your Prayers." January 1965: 6.
"Nat Cole, John Wayne: The Whole World Prays. . . . " April 1956:
          15.
"Around the Lots." June 1956: 70.
"He Feels Fine, But. . . . " October 1965: 832.
"3 Marriages, 7 Children, 10 Grandchildren, 200 films and 2 lives
          later . . . : The Incredible Life Story of John Wayne." Octo-
          ber 1966: 32–37.
"Hollywood Dateline." January 1967: 8.
"Hot Off the Teletype." February 1967: 8.
"Hollywood Dateline." March 1967: 10.
Austin, John. "Oxygen Rushed to John Wayne." September 1967:
          28–29, 57.
"Why Hollywood Parents Live in Constant Fear." November 1967:
          42–43, 68–70.

Feinstein, Phyllis. "Some Guys Never Learn." February 1968: 26–27, 59–61.

Sasso, Joey. "How Big, Brawling John Wayne Fights Pornography." May 1970: 29–30, 62–64.

"Big John Wayne's Secret For Staying Young?" June 1970: 28–29.

"John Wayne's Shocking Confession: 'I Believe in White Supremacy.' " September 1971: 26, 60.

Colbert, Arthur. "John Wayne Hoax Revealed." December 1977: 34–35, 60–62.

Steele, Sam. "John Wayne Faces Accusers: 'Don't Call Me a Racist Pig!' " November 1973: 36–37, 58–61.

"The John Waynes to Divorce!" March 1974: 54.

"The John Waynes Together Again!" December 1974: 52.

Catt, Charlie. "The Woman Who Can't Love John Wayne Enough." April 1977: 26, 48.

*Movie Show* (volumes 1–6, October 1942–June 1948)

"Flying Tigers." October 1942: 46–47.

"Pittsburgh." January 1943: 14–15.

"In Old Oklahoma." December 1943: 34–35.

"The Fighting Seabees." April 1944: 34–35.

Bangs, Bee. " 'I Owe a Lot to Friends.' " December 1944: 28–29, 60.

"Flame of the Barbary Coast." June 1945: 44–45.

"With the Invisible Army." July 1945: 62.

"Without Reservations." May 1946: 40.

"The Angel and the Badman." March 1947: 66.

Color portrait April 1947: 38.

"Tycoon." December 1947: 52.

"Fort Apache." May 1948: 36.

*Movie Stars* (*Parade*) (volumes 2, 5–30, December 1941–November 1942; December 1944–September 1978; 1973 and 1975 incomplete)

"Reap the Wild Wind." June 1942: 22–23.

"Howdy Duke." January 1946: 32–33, 79.

"The Duke Produces." March 1947: 22–23.

"Tall in the Saddle." November 1949: 48–49.

St. Johns, Adela Rogers. "The Real John Wayne." August 1950: 48–49, 82–84.

"John Wayne in *Jet Pilot*." May 1951: 43.

"Heading Up." June 1951: 56–57.

Weller, Helen Hover. "The High Cost of Hollywood Love." March 1953: 54–55.

"Wayne's Woes." August 1953: 16–17.

"John Wayne in *The High and the Mighty*." February 1954: 54.

Phillips, Dee. "John Wayne: Why Hollywood Swears By Him—and at Him." November 1954: 40–41, 59.

"Listen, Son." March 1955: 42–53, 74–76.

"Do Married Men Make the Best Lovers?" August 1955: 35–37.

"When Is A Lover Too Old?—John Wayne." November 1957: 46.

"John Wayne" (wallet pic and capsule biography). July 1959: 41.

"Hollywood Who's Who." February 1960: 39.

"Hollywood Hot Heads." October 1960: 30.

"They've Come a Long, Long Way." July 1962: 41.

"What It's Like to Be Married to Hollywood's Most Virile Husband . . . by Mrs. John Wayne." March 1965: 42–43, 75–79.

"Revealed: Which Hollywood Husbands Stay Faithful." May 1963: 33.

"Hollywood Husbands and their 'Backstreet' Wives." February 1964: 41.

"Hidden Tragedies of Hollywood's Children." March 1964: 18.

"The Special Sex Appeal of Older Men." June 1964: 14.

"All Star Pin-ups." April 1965: 74.

"John Wayne's Three Miracles." June 1965: 20, 22–25.

"Pat Wayne's Wedding." March 1966: 26–27.

Courtney, Stewart. "Hollywood Turns Pagan." June 1968: 32–33, 67–70.

"John Wayne: Forever Papa." November 1968: 30–32.

"The Indestructible Duke." November 1969: 32–33, 49.

Ross, Marilyn T. "They're Never Too Old!" September 1970: 44–51.

Elwood, Roger. "John Wayne's Religion." September 1971: 34–35, 57, 60.

Cameron, Sue. "The Story Behind The John Waynes' Split! Why This 'Perfect Marriage' Failed!" March 1974: 27, 70, 72.

"His 'High Noon' at Harvard." May 1974: 44–45, 66.

Walker, Janet. "John Wayne Has That New Operation To Satisfy His Young Love." July 1975: 28–29, 48–50.

*The New Movie Magazine* (volumes 1–12, December
1929–September 1935)

Blair, Harry N. "3 Boys Who Won." February 1931: 51, 121.

*Photoplay Magazine* (volumes 1–91, 1911–June
1977; including *Movie Mirror*, volumes 1–17,
1931–1940, merged with *Photoplay* in 1941)

Hughes, M. "Oh, For a Hair Cut!" December 1930: 45.
Asher, Jerry. "Devil-May-Care!" *Movie Mirror*, June 1939: 45,
88–89.
Reid, Sally. " 'Mother' Wayne." October 1940: 26, 97.
Sharpe, H. "John the Duke." January 1944: 47–48.
West, R. "Measure of a Man." November 1944: 58.
Waterbury, Ruth. "Sunrise Serenade (Mr. and Mrs. John Wayne)."
June 1946: 31, 80–81.
Howe, H. "Duke in Coonskin." January 1950: 54.
Ford, J. "Man Alive!" March 1951: 42.
Connolly, M. and E. Ford. "Secrets Behind Hollywood Heartaches."
November 1952: 46.
Armstrong, G. "The Duke Takes A Stand." September 1953: 33.
Armstrong, G. "The Story John Wayne Has Never Told." October
1953: 38.
Stack, R. "Duke—Prince Among Men." April 1955: 54.
Hoffman, J. "Night of Terror." May 1958: 70.
Watson, B. "Daddy, When Will God Bring My Baby Brother?"
October 1959: 44.
Dawes, A. "Glamous Grandfather." December 1962: 56.
Corbin, Julia. "Big Man! Big Life! Big Love!" October 1963: 34–35.
Wayne, John, as told to George Carpozi. "How I Conquered Cancer."
April 1965: 62–63, 93–94.
Tusher, Bill. "The Son Who Made Him Cry." August 1965: 46–48,
78–79.
Allen, Carol. "Sure I've Sinned, But. . . . " January 1966: 21–23,
59–60.
Tusher, Will. "His Miracle Baby." June 1966: 44–49.
Tusher, Will. "Why I Had to Go To Vietnam." October 1966: 40–43,
78–79.

O'Brien, Fred. "What Do Men Talk About When There Are No Women Around?" July 1967: 50–51, 80.

Tusher, William. "My Helpless, Hopeless, Heavenly Husband." November 1967: 35–37, 75.

Terry, Polly. "Letters That Make John Wayne Cry." September 1968: 33–35, 96–97.

Ardmore, Jane. "John Wayne & His Women in Every Port!" April 1969: 40–41, 79–81.

Thorpe, Jay. "Playing with Death." December 1969: 59–60.

Roberts, Harry. " 'I Can't Love A Woman Enough!' " March 1970: 42–43, 93–94.

Conner, Peg. "His Wife's Story." May 1970: 48–49, 97–99. (Cover story of "Super Father of the Year")

Trumpler, Liselotte. "Wife's Strange Confession." September 1970: 52–53, 103–105.

"John Wayne Has Twins." December 1970: 40–43.

Paxton, Steve. "John Wayne's Screaming Battles with His Wife." February 1971: 52–53, 106, 108.

Gregory, James. "What John Wayne Tells His Children About Drugs . . . Hippies . . . the War . . . Sex. . . . " July 1971: 80–81, 124–126.

Tusher, Will. "The Waynes and Mitchums: What the Sons Say About Their Fathers." November 1971: 82–87, 121–127.

Gregory, Jim. "The Calm Years Are Wild." March 1972: 42–45, 8–9.

"*Photoplay's* 51st Gold Medal Awards." September 1972: 52–54.

Gregory, James. "Boyhood Memories." November 1972: 38–39, 69–70.

Kane, Tom, as told to May Mann. "John Wayne Saved My Life!" May 1973: 28, 33, 35, 45.

Mann, May. "The Burtons and the Waynes Argue: The Right and the Wrong Way to Love." May 1973: 54–59, 96–98.

Ardmore, Jane. "Frantic John Wayne Rushes His Wife to Hospital." May 1973: 60, 71.

Tusher, Will. " 'John Wayne Made Me More of a Woman.' " June 1973: 60–61, 84–91.

Terry, Polly. "John Wayne Weeps for the Lost Child He Loved." August 1973: 70–71, 82.

Treolar, Dorothy. "Maureen O'Hara Answers—What Makes John Wayne Hollywood's Favorite Lover?" October 1973: 44–45, 66, 69.

Reynolds, Lisa. "The Day the Cops Arrested Me." November 1973: 54–55, 57, 60.

Ardmore, Jane. " 'I Won't Divorce Duke!' " December 1973: 12, 15, 84–85.

Ardmore, Jane. " 'My Dad, John Wayne.' " February 1974: 50–51, 109–114.

Ardmore, Jane. "John Wayne's Wife Tells Why They've Split." February 1974: 52–54, 114.

Ardmore, Jane. "The John Waynes in Each Other's Arms Again." April 1974: 32, 45–46.

Tusher, Will. "First She Loses Duke . . . and Now Her Daughter." November 1974: 46, 80–82.

Tusher, Will. "John Wayne Coughing Up Blood!" August 1974: 46–47, 70, 74.

Tusher, Will. " 'I'm Trying Not to Make an Idiot of Myself!' " June 1975: 18, 34.

Tusher, Will. "How Much Can A Human Body Endure?" September 1975: 60, 78–80.

Ardmore, Jane. "What It's Like to Work for A Superstar." August 1976: 18–19, 67–70.

Francis, Carl. "If I Had My Life to Live Over Again." December 1976: 26–28.

Ardmore, Jane. "My Daddy, John Wayne." May 1977: 16, 74.

*Picture Play* (volumes 1–53, April 1915–February 1941; thereafter *Charm*)

"Favorites of the Fans." March 1937: 71.
"On Location with *Stagecoach*." March 1939: 52–53.

*Screen* (volumes 1–4, May 1953–November 1956)

Canfield, Alyce. "Not Meant For Love." May 1953: 13–16, 68, 70, 72.

James, Walker. "Is Marriage Just a Love Trap for . . . John Wayne?" March 1954: 12–16, 72–73.

*Screen Guide* (volume 1–15, May 1936–1950)

"Reap the Wild Wind—Award of Merit Film." May 1942: 26–27.
"Hollywood Springs a Surprise!—*Lady Takes a Chance.*" August
1943: 24–25.
"John Wayne Comes Home." June 1944: 38.
Color Portrait. November 1945: 33.
Cummings, John. "The Facts Behind His Meteoric Rise to Popular-
ity." May 1950: 62–65.
Color Photo. August 1950: 50.

*Screenland* (volumes 5–69, September
1922–December 1970)

Tildesley, Ruth. "Our 1931 Catalogue of Bachelors." January 1931:
64–65, 128.
"Stars As They Are: Exclusive Portraits by Cecil Beaton." June 1931:
48.
Adams, Sam. "Re-Discovered!" October 1939: 63, 82–83.
"Don't Call Him 'Cowboy'!" December 1940: 45.
"Live and Let Love." May 1941: 46.
Peterson, Elizabeth B. (fictionalization by). "*In Old California.*" June
1942: 30–31, 46–49.
Liza. "Closeup of A Cowboy." January 1944: 41, 89.
Color portrait from *In Old California.* January 1944: 40.
Hall, Gladys. "The Anti-Phony." January 1946: 24–25, 65–66.
"Glory for John." June 1950: 44.
"Cold War Romance." September 1950: 39.
Wayne, Mrs. John. "Almost a 'Movie Widow.' " December 1950:
36–37, 60–61.
Lane, Frances. "Inside Story on the John Wayne Split-Up." Novem-
ber 1952: 30–31, 58–61.
Reid, Louis. "John's Incurable Complex." August 1953: 36–37,
62–63.
Reid, Louis. "Ghosts of the John Wayne Divorce Case." April 1954:
24–25, 56–57.
Wayne, Patrick. "Don't Tangle With My Dad." March 1955: 44–47,
70.
Pine, Dick. "John Takes the Stand." January 1956: 22–25, 69–70.
"Out West with the Duke." May 1956: 30–33.

Tusher, William. "The Biggest Daddy of Them All." January 1965: 32–35, 51–52.

Kesselman, Judi R. "His Miracle Baby." January 1966: 28–29, 56–57.

Cronin, Jeff. "Why John Wayne's Wife Is So Terrified For His Life." February 1970: 28–31, 49–50.

Dinter, Charlotte. "John Wayne's Secret Proposal to Jackie: 'Your Yacht—Or Mine?' " May 1970: 16–19.

*Screen Life* (volumes 6–7, May 1953–January 1955; Misbound as volumes 8–9)

"The Secret That Makes 'Duke' King." September 1953: 24–27.

"He Doesn't Give A Hoot." July 1954: 50–51.

*Screen Stars* (volumes 1–35, April 1944–1977; 1972, 1974, 1977 incomplete)

Pin-up: "John Wayne" (from *Tall in the Saddle*). February 1945: 50.

Stuart, Lila. "Regular Guy." August 1945: 34–35, 76–77.

Holland, Jack. "The Kind of Wife John Wayne Needs." June 1954: 16–17, 76–77.

Wayne, Toni. "I Call Him Dad." May 1955: 36–37, 64, 66.

"They Call Him Duke!" August 1964: 22–23, 64–65.

Vande Paer, Lisa. "John Wayne—What Keeps Him At the Top?" August 1966: 60–61, 81–82.

Elwood, Roger. " 'I Thank God I'm Alive.' " November 1969: 46–49, 84–86.

"Behind the Scenes with John Wayne in *Chisum*." August 1970: 50–51.

Graves, Victoria. " 'I'm Just a Half-Drunken Old Man!' " September 1970: 52–53, 62, 66.

Storm, Robin. " 'I Don't Understand Women.' " March 1971: 32–33, 76–78.

Amir, Fanuk. " 'I've Lost My Little Girl!' " February 1972: 52–53, 79–80.

Dantes, Susanna. "Only John Wayne Knows the Horror Ann-Margret is Forced to Endure. . . ." November 1972: 36–37, 86–87.

Chapman, Penelope. "Armed Guards Called in To Protect John Wayne." May 1974: 42–43, 66–68.

Wilson, Dave. "John Wayne: A Hollywood Legend." August 1974:
    32–34, 85–86, and September 1974: 52–53, 66–68.

*Silver Screen* (volumes 1–42, November
    1930–October 1972)

Babcock, Gladys. "On Location with the *Stagecoach* Troupe." March
    1939: 26–27, 68–71.
"We Point With Pride To: John Wayne." October 1940: 50.
Reid, James. "From Mustang to Marlene!" November 1940: 26–27,
    76–78.
Manners, Mary Jane. "Fool-Proof Marriage Insurance." September
    1942: 26–27, 60–62.
"*A Lady Takes a Chance.*" July 1943: 33.
Wilson, Elizabeth. "He's the Hottest Thing in Pictures Today!"
    December 1943: 26–27, 84–85.
Bangs, Bee. "They Grew Up Together." October 1945: 42–43, 80–
    82.
Palmer, Constance. "Big Business is His Hobby." July 1947: 45,
    77–78.
"The John Waynes at Home." March 1948: 48–49.
Wilson, Elizabeth. "History Repeats Itself and How!" February 1950:
    30–31, 58–60.
Barnett, Bev. "No Overnight Sensation." August 1951: 42–43, 65–68.
Cox, Sallie Belle. "The Male Point of View." June 1953: 28–29,
    61–62.
Palette, Pilar. " 'My Husband John Wayne.' " August 1955: 40–45.
Wayne, Pat. "My Old Man." October 1957: 58–53.
Wayne, Pilar. "Confessions of a Movie Idol's Wife." April 1958:
    15–17, 63, 71–72.
"Bravo, Duke." October 1959: 26–27.
"It's Baby Time in the Old School." January 1966: 16–17.
Lewis, Amy. "My Dad is Duke Wayne." September 1966: 26–29,
    52–54.
Borie, Marcia. "The Last of the Lonesome Cowboys." July 1969:
    46–47, 54–56.
Cameron, Claire. "The One War John Won't Fight." October 1969:
    36–37, 46–48.
Cronin, Jeff. "Revealed: The Death Plot Against John!" May 1970:
    42–43, 46–47.

James, Foster. "John Wayne Faces Cancer—Again!" November 1970: 36–39, 44–45.

Friedman, Favius. "Mother Hen." April 1971: 40–43, 47.

Perry, Jennifer. "Mrs. John Wayne Talks About Her Most Terrible Fears for Her Family." May 1971: 40–41, 46.

## MISCELLANEOUS NONPRINT SOURCES

### Radio

*Three Sheets to the Wind*. Director Tay Garnett. 26 thirty-minute episodes. NBC, 1942, 1943. Scripts in the USC collection (see Archival Materials). Wayne stars as detective-spy on an ocean cruise who covers his investigation by posing as a drunk.

*Screen Director's Playhouse* (original title *NBC Theatre*). NBC, 1949 and later. Radio versions of famous films, featuring introductory interviews with the directors, stars. Wayne starred in the opening show, *Stagecoach*, January 9, 1949, and in later show, *Fort Apache*.

### Records

*101 Strings Presents a Tribute to John Wayne*. 1980

Morgan, Geof. *It Comes with the Plumbing*. Nexus Records, Nashville, Tenn., n.d. Feminist men's music, featuring a song titled, "Goodbye, John Wayne."

Wayne, John. *America, Why I Love Her*. RCA, LSP-4828, 1973.

### Television

*The Beverly Hillbillies*. CBS 19 August 1967.

"The Colter Craven Story." Director John Ford. *Wagon Train*. NBC, 23 November 1960.

"Flashing Spikes." Director John Ford. *Alcoa Premiere*, ABC, 4 October 1962.

*General Electric All-Star Anniversary Show*. CBS, 29 September 1978.

"Host the Third Side." *The Dick Powell Theatre*. NBC, 26 March 1963.

*Legends of the West.* CBS, 1981.
"Lucy and John Wayne." *I Love Lucy.* CBS, 10 October 1955.
*The Lucy Show.* CBS, 21 November 1966.
"John Wayne and I." *The Merv Show.* November 1980. Merv Griffin
    interviews director Andrew McLaughlin
*Maude.* CBS, 9 September 1974.
*Oscar Presents the War Movies and John Wayne.* NBC, 1977.
"Rookie of the Year." Director John Ford. *Screen Directors Play-
    house.* NBC, 7 December 1955.
*Sing Out, Sweet Land.* NBC, November 1970.
Wayne also appeared as a guest on variety shows, among them, *The
    Red Skelton Show, The Dean Martin Show,* Bob Hope Spe-
    cials, and *Laugh-in.* Indexes to network news programs cite
    coverage of Wayne, including specials done when he died.


**Memorabilia**

Among many "memorial" items which appeared after Wayne's death:
John Wayne Commemorative Medal Belt Buckle. Nancy Allen Co.,
    Westport, Connecticut.
John Wayne Limited Edition Ceramic Bust Decanter. (Several distrib-
    utors).
John Wayne Memorial Medal. The American Treasury Mint, Phila-
    delphia, Pennsylvania. The Historic Providence Mint, Provi-
    dence, Rhode Island.
"The Man of the Golden West." Commemorative plate by Endre
    Szabo for Lynell Studio Collection, 1976.


## ARCHIVAL MATERIALS

Many library and institutional collections contain materials relevant
to Wayne's career. The following is a distillation of collections listed
in two very useful references: Nancy Allen's *Film Study Collections:
A Guide to their Development and Use* (New York: Unger, 1979) and
Linda Harris Mehr's *Motion Pictures, Television and Radio: A Union
Catalogue of Manuscript and Special Collections in the Western
United States* (Boston: G. K. Hall, 1977).

Not included in this listing are the many U.S. government archives which would contain records of Wayne's political correspondence and dealings with government agencies. See Bonnie G. Rowan's *Scholar's Guide to Washington, D.C., Film and Video Collections* (DC: Woodrow Wilson International Center for Scholars, Smithsonian Institution Press, 1980) for valuable suggestions on tracking down paper records. Helpful, too, is the appendix to Lawrence Suid's *Guts and Glory*, which gives information on the records of Wayne and the military.

Academy of Motion Picture Arts and Sciences
Margaret Herrick Library
8949 Wilshire Blvd.
Beverly Hills, CA 90211
(213) 278-4313

Extensive Paramount materials, 1926-1970; Universal materials 1945-55; and scripts from Paramount, RKO, and DeMille productions. Mehr also lists set design papers for *The Fighting Seabees* in the Duncan Cramer Collection. Also a magazine index to over sixty titles, including their complete *Photoplay* collection.

American Film Institute
Charles K. Feldman Library
501 Doheny Road
Beverly Hills, CA 90210

A large script collection, including final screenplay and shooting script of *The Shootist*; production design for *The Shootist*; transcripts of oral history series including interviews of Allen Dwan, Henry Fonda, and Howard Hawks; Time-Life series Audio History series, including Wayne and many he worked with; Henry Hathaway papers, 1932-1968, including shooting scripts.

Arizona Historical Society
949 East Second Street
Tucson, AZ 85719
(602) 882-5774

Oral history collection of filmmakers working in Arizona, including Wayne and many associates (Bruce Cabot, Yakima Canutt, William Clothier, Howard Hawks, Ben Johnson, Chuck Roberson, Hal Taliaferro); also a supporting clipping file.

Burbank Public Library
Warner Research Collection
110 North Glenoaks Boulevard
Burbank, CA 91503
(213) 847-9743.

Warner Brothers papers and memorabilia of 1930's-40's.

George Eastman House
Film Department
900 East Avenue
Rochester, NY 14607
(716) 271-3361

M-G-M Collection and Cecil B. DeMille Estate Collection. Early westerns; stills from Warners, M-G-M; film collection.

Georgetown University Library
Special Collections
37th and O Streets, NW
Washington, D.C. 20057
(202) 625-3230

Oral history interviews done by Lawrence Suid for his book, *Guts and Glory*, including Wayne and son Michael Wayne on *The Green Berets* and several military and government officials who advised Wayne war films. See Suid's book for a complete listing.

Glendale Public Library
Department of Special Collections
222 East Harvard St.
Glendale, CA 91205
(213) 956-2037.

RKO scripts from 1934-1941.

Museum of Modern Art
Department of Film
Film Study Center
11 West 53rd Street
New York, NY 10019
(212) 708-9613

Film collection, including among others, a decent print of *The Big Trail*; Allied Artists and Republic scripts; audio tapes of film makers; clipping files; stills collection.

National Cowboy Hall of Fame and Western Heritage Center
1700 NE 63rd
Oklahoma City, Oklahoma
(405) 478-2250

Wayne donated a collection of 230 items of his memorabilia worth $3 million in 1979, including guns, saddles, art work.

University of California, Los Angeles
Film, Television, and Radio Archives
Department of Theater Arts
University of California at Los Angeles
Los Angeles, California 90024
(213) 825-4880, 825-4988, 825-4879

12,000 film titles, including Paramount 1930's-40's, Republic 1930's-40's, 20th Century Fox 1920's-60's, Warner Brothers 1930's-40's. 20,000 TV programs from 1947; 10,000 radio transcriptions from 1930's.

Theater Arts Library
University of California, Los Angeles
Los Angeles, CA 90024
(213) 825-4880.

UCLA University Research Library
Department of Special Collections

The Library contains scripts of Fox, 20th-Century Fox, M-G-M; radio and TV scripts; many stills and publicity collections. It also acquired three decades of RKO scripts and production files.

The Special Collections house all major paper materials of the University of California at Los Angeles, including the continuity and shooting scripts of Republic Pictures; Mirisch Production files; the papers of Wayne's immediate associates Dudley Nichols, Alen LeMay, Kenneth Gamet, and Russell Birdwell. Both the Special Collections and the Theater Arts Library have extensive oral history tapes.

University of Southern California
Doheny Library
University Park
Los Angeles, California 90089
(213) 741-6058.

Large collections of taped interviews, stills, publicity materials, clipping files, and scripts. Universal Studio's collection and Warner Brothers-Burbank files. Many personal papers; of note are those of Tay Garnett, containing scripts of *Three Sheets to the Wind* radio series, and Albert Lewin, containing correspondence with Wayne.

University of Texas-Austin
Hoblitzelle Theatre Arts Library
Humanities Research Center
P. O. Box 7219
Austin, Texas 78712
(512) 471-9122

Scripts and publicity collections. Maurice Zolotow Collection of interviews, including those done for the biography of Wayne.

Wisconsin Center for Film and Theater Research
University of Wisconsin-Madison
6039 Vilas Communication Hall
Madison, WI 53706
(608) 262-9706

Film Archive
State Historical Society
816 State St.
Madison, WI 53706
(608) 262-3338

The University and Historical Society holdings constitute joint archives containing: graphics and promotional materials, especially M-G-M, Warner Brothers, Universal, Republic and United Artists; film collection, notably RKO and Monogram of 1930's-40's; television shows of 1940's-60's; many special collections of individuals and companies, notably that of Walter Mirisch.

# APPENDIX A:
# JOHN WAYNE
# FILMOGRAPHY

The exact number of John Wayne's film appearances remains elusive; counting each chapter of his thirties' serials as a separate movie, the total hits around 186 films. His early work at Fox is difficult to confirm. Wayne himself has been quoted as claiming a sequence as a double for Francis X. Bushman in *Brown of Harvard* (1926) as his first appearance. His role as an unbilled extra in *Mother Machree* is disputed, but he is known to have propped for Ford on that film, so there is some likelihood he worked as an extra, too. *Hangman's House* clearly shows young Wayne in a short sequence, so the film is often given as his first. This filmography does not include Wayne's film work as narrator or in walk-on roles. See the discussion of filmographies in chapter 4 for more information on these. Also, this filmography is skeletal; full listings of credits and casts can be found in book-length filmographies, notably Eyles's.

*The Drop Kick*; Year released: 1927; Directed by: Millard Webb; Produced by: First National; Role: Extra as Football Player.
*Mother Machree*; Year released: 1928; Directed by: John Ford; Produced by: Fox Film Studios; Role: Unbilled extra.
*Hangman's House*; Year released: 1928; Directed by: John Ford; Produced by: Fox; Role: Horse-Race Spectator.
*Words and Music*; Year released: 1929; Directed by: James Tinling; Produced by: Fox; Role: Pete Donahue (Billed as Duke Morrison)

*Salute*; Year released: 1929; Directed by: John Ford; Produced by:
Fox; Role: Football Player
*Men Without Women*; Year released: 1930; Directed by: John Ford;
Produced by: Fox; Role: Crew Member.
*Rough Romance*; Year released: 1930; Directed by: A. F. Erickson;
Produced by: Fox; Role: Bit Player
*Cheer Up and Smile*; Year released: 1930; Directed by: Sidney
Lanfield; Produced by: Fox; Role: Bit Player
*The Big Trail*; Year released: 1930; Directed by: Raoul Walsh;
Produced by: Fox; Role: Breck Coleman
*Three Girls Lost*; Year released: 1931; Directed by: Sidney Lanfield;
Produced by: Fox; Role: Gordon Wales
*Girls Demand Excitement*; Year released: 1931; Directed by: Sey-
mour Felix; Produced by: Fox; Role: Peter Brooks
*Men Are Like That*; Year released: 1931; Directed by: George B.
Seitz; Produced by: Columbia; Role: Lt. Bob Denton
*Range Feud*; Year released: 1931; Directed by: D. Ross Lederman;
Produced by: Columbia; Role: Clint Turner
*Maker of Men*; Year released: 1931; Directed by: Edward Sedgwick;
Produced by: Columbia; Role: Dusty
*Shadow of the Eagle* (serial); Year released: 1932; Directed by: Ford
Beebe; Produced by: Nat Levine/Mascot; Role: Craig McCoy
*Texas Cyclone*; Year released: 1932; Directed by: D. Ross Lederman;
Produced by: Columbia; Role: Steve Pickett
*Two Fisted Law*; Year released: 1932; Directed by: D. Ross Leder-
man; Produced by: Columbia; Role: Duke
*Lady and Gent*; Year released: 1932; Directed by: Stephen Roberts;
Produced by: Paramount; Role: Buzz Kinney
*The Hurricane Express* (serial); Year released: 1932; Directed by:
Armand Schaefer and J. P. McGowan; Produced by: Nat
Levine/Mascot; Role: Larry Baker
*Ride Him Cowboy*; Year released: 1932; Directed by: Fred Allen;
Produced by: Warner Bros.; Role: John Drury
*The Big Stampede*; Year released: 1932; Directed by: Tenny Wright;
Produced by: Warner Bros.; Role: John Steele
*Haunted Gold*; Year released: 1932; Directed by: Mack V. Wright;
Produced by: Warner Bros.; Role: John Mason
*The Telegraph Trail*; Year released: 1933; Directed by: Tenny
Wright; Produced by: Warner Bros.; Role: John Trent

*The Three Musketeers* (serial); Year released: 1933; Directed by: Armand Schaefer; Produced by: Mascot; Role: Tom Wayne

*Central Airport*; Year released: 1933; Directed by: William A. Wellman; Produced by: Warner Bros.; Role: Man in Wreck

*Somewhere in Sonora*; Year released: 1933; Directed by: Mack V. Wright; Produced by: Warner Bros.; Role: John Bishop

*His Private Secretary*; Year released: 1933; Directed by: Philip B. Whitman; Produced by: Showmen's Pictures; Role: Dick Wallace

*The Life of Jimmy Dolan*; Year released: 1933; Directed by: Archie Mayo; Produced by: Warner Bros.; Role: Smith

*Baby Face*; Year released: 1933; Directed by Alfred E. Green; Produced by: Warner Bros.; Role: Jimmy McCoy

*The Man From Monterey*; Year released: 1933; Directed by: Mack V. Wright; Produced by: Warner Bros.; Role: Captain John Holmes

*Riders of Destiny*; Year released: 1933; Directed by: R. N. Bradbury; Produced by: Lone Star; Role: Sandy Saunders ("Singin' Sandy")

*College Coach*; Year released: 1933; Directed by: William A. Wellman; Produced by: Warner Bros.; Role: Bit Player

*Sagebrush Trail*; Year released: 1933; Directed by: Armand Schaefer; Produced by: Paul Malvern/Lone Star; Role: John Brant

*The Lucky Texan*; Year released: 1934; Directed by: Robert N. Bradbury; Produced by: Paul Malvern/Lone Star; Role: Jerry Mason

*West of the Divide*; Year released: 1934; Directed by: Robert N. Bradbury; Produced by: Paul Malvern/Lone Star; Role: Ted Hayden

*Blue Steel*; Year released: 1934; Directed by: Robert N. Bradbury; Produced by: Paul Malvern/Lone Star; Role: John Carruthers

*The Man From Utah*; Year released: 1934; Directed by: Robert N. Bradbury; Produced by: Paul Malvern/Lone Star; Role: John Weston

*Randy Rides Alone*; Year released: 1934; Directed by: Harry Fraser; Produced by: Paul Malvern/Lone Star; Role: Randy Bowers

*The Star Packer*; Year released: 1934; Directed by: Robert N. Bradbury; Produced by: Paul Malvern/Lone Star; Role: John Travers

*The Trail Beyond*; Year released: 1934; Directed by: Robert N. Bradbury;
    Produced by: Paul Malvern/Lone Star; Role: Rod Drew
*The Lawless Frontier*; Year released: 1934; Directed by: Robert N.
    Bradbury; Produced by: Paul Malvern/Lone Star; Role: John
    Tobin
*'Neath Arizona Skies*; Year released: 1934; Directed by: Harry Fra-
    ser; Produced by: Paul Malvern/Lone Star; Role: Chris
    Morrell
*Texas Terror*; Year released: 1935; Directed by: Robert N. Bradbury;
    Produced by: Paul Malvern/Lone Star; Role: John Higgins
*Rainbow Valley*; Year released: 1935; Directed by: Robert N. Brad-
    bury; Produced by: Paul Malvern/Lone Star; Role: John
    Martin
*The Desert Trail*; Year released: 1935; Directed by: Cullen Lewis;
    Produced by: Paul Malvern/Lone Star; Role: John Scott
*The Dawn Rider*; Year released: 1935; Directed by: Robert N. Brad-
    bury; Produced by: Paul Malvern/Monogram; Role: John
    Mason
*Paradise Canyon*; Year released: 1935; Directed by: Carl Pierson;
    Produced by: Paul Malvern/Monogram; Role: John Wyatt
*Western Ho*; Year released: 1935; Directed by: Robert N. Bradbury;
    Produced by: Paul Malvern/Republic; Role: John Wyatt
*The New Frontier*; Year released: 1935; Directed by: Carl Pierson;
    Produced by: Paul Malvern/Republic; Role: John Dawson
*The Lawless Range*; Year released: 1935; Directed by: Robert N.
    Bradbury; Produced by: Trem Carr/Republic; Role: John
    Middleton
*The Oregon Trail*; Year released: 1936; Directed by: Scott Pembroke;
    Produced by: Paul Malvern/Republic; Role: Captain John
    Delmont
*The Lawless Nineties*; Year released: 1936; Directed by: Joseph Kane;
    Produced by: Republic; Role: John Tipton
*King of the Pecos*; Year released: 1936; Directed by: Joseph Kane;
    Produced by: Republic; Role: John Clayborn
*The Lonely Trail*; Year released: 1936; Directed by: Joseph Kane;
    Produced by: Nat Levine/Republic; Role: John
*Winds of the Wasteland*; Year released: 1936; Directed by: Mack V.
    Wright; Produced by: Nat Levine/Republic; Role: John Blair

*The Sea Spoilers*; Year released: 1936; Directed by: Frank Strayer; Produced by: Trem Carr/Universal; Role: Bob Randall

*Conflict*; Year released: 1936; Directed by: David Howard; Produced by: Trem Carr/Universal; Role: Pat

*California Straight Ahead*; Year released: 1937; Directed by: Arthur Lubin; Produced by: Trem Carr/Universal; Role: Biff Smith

*I Cover the War*; Year released: 1937; Directed by: Arthur Lubin; Produced by: Trem Carr/Universal; Role: Bob Adams

*Idol of the Crowds*; Year released: 1937; Directed by: Arthur Lubin; Produced by: Trem Carr/Universal; Role: Johnny Hanson

*Adventure's End*; Year released: 1937; Directed by: Arthur Lubin; Produced by: Trem Carr/Universal; Role: Duke Slade

*Born to the West*; Year released: 1937; Directed by: Charles Barton; Produced by: Paramount; Role: Dare Rudd

*Pals of the Saddle*; Year released: 1938; Directed by: George Sherman; Produced by: Republic; Role: Stony Brooke

*Overland Stage Raiders*; Year released: 1938; Directed by: George Sherman; Produced by: Republic; Role: Stony Brooke

*Santa Fe Stampede*; Year released: 1938; Directed by: George Sherman; Produced by: Republic; Role: Stony Brooke

*Red River Range*; Year released: 1938; Directed by: George Sherman; Produced by: Republic; Role: Stony Brooke

*Stagecoach*; Year released: 1939; Directed by: John Ford; Produced by: Walter Wanger Productions; Role: The Ringo Kid

*The Night Riders*; Year released: 1939; Directed by: George Sherman; Produced by: Republic; Role: Stony Brooke

*Three Texas Steers*; Year released: 1939; Directed by: George Sherman; Produced by: Republic; Role: Stony Brooke

*Wyoming Outlaw*; Year released: 1939; Directed by: George Sherman; Produced by: Republic; Role: Stony Brooke

*New Frontier*; Year released: 1939; Directed by: George Sherman; Produced by: Republic; Role: Stony Brooke

*Allegheny Uprising*; Year released: 1939; Directed by: William A. Seiter; Produced by: P. J. Wolfson/RKO Radio; Role: Jim Smith

*The Dark Command*; Year released: 1940; Directed by: Raoul Walsh; Produced by: Republic; Role: Bob Seton

*Three Faces West*; Year released: 1940; Directed by: Bernard Vorhaus; Produced by: Republic; Role: John Philips

*The Long Voyage Home*; Year released: 1940; Directed by: John
    Ford; Produced by: Walter Wanger; Role: Ole Olsen
*Seven Sinners*; Year released: 1940; Directed by: Tay Garnett; Pro-
    duced by: Joe Pasternak/Universal; Role: Lieutenant Dan
    Brent
*A Man Betrayed*; Year released: 1941; Directed by: John H. Auer;
    Produced by: Republic; Role: Lynn Hollister
*Lady From Louisiana*; Year released: 1941; Directed by: Bernard
    Vorhaus; Produced by: Republic; Role: John Reynolds
*The Shepherd of the Hills*; Year released: 1941; Directed by: Henry
    Hathaway; Produced by: Jack Moss/Paramount; Role: Matt
    Matthews
*Lady For A Night*; Year released: 1942; Directed by: Leigh Jason;
    Produced by: Republic; Role: Jack Morgan
*Reap the Wild Wind*; Year released: 1942; Directed by: Cecil B.
    DeMille; Produced by: Paramount; Role: Captain Jack Stuart
*The Spoilers*; Year released: 1942; Directed by: Ray Enright; Pro-
    duced by: Frank Lloyd/Charles K. Feldman Group; Role:
    Roy Glennister
*In Old California*; Year released: 1942; Directed by: William
    McGann; Produced by: Republic; Role: Tom Craig
*Flying Tigers*; Year released: 1942; Directed by: David Miller; Pro-
    duced by: Republic; Role: Jim Gordon
*Reunion in France*; Year released: 1942; Directed by: Jules Dassin;
    Produced by: Joseph L. Mankiewicz/M-G-M; Role: Pat Tal-
    bot
*Pittsburgh*; Year released: 1942; Directed by: Louis Seiler; Produced
    by: Robert Fellows/Charles K. Feldman Group; Role: Charles
    "Pittsburgh" Markham
*A Lady Takes a Chance*; Year released: 1943; Directed by: William
    A. Seiter; Produced by: Frank Ross/RKO Radio; Role: Duke
    Hudkins
*In Old Oklahoma*; Year released: 1943; Directed by: Albert S. Rogell;
    Produced by: Republic; Role: Dan Somers
*The Fighting Seabees*; Year released: 1944; Directed by: Edward
    Ludwig; Produced by: Republic; Role: Wedge Donovan
*Tall in the Saddle*; Year released: 1944; Directed by: Edwin L. Marin;
    Produced by: Robert Fellows/RKO Radio; Role: Rocklin

*Flame of the Barbary Coast*; Year released: 1945; Directed by: Joseph Kane; Produced by: Republic; Role: Duke Fergus

*Back to Bataan*; Year released: 1945; Directed by: Edward Dmytryk; Produced by: Robert Fellows/RKO Radio; Role: Colonel Joseph Madden

*They Were Expendable*; Year released: 1945; Directed by: John Ford; Produced by: John Ford/M-G-M; Role: Lieutenant Rusty Ryan

*Dakota*; Year released: 1945; Directed by: Joseph Kane; Produced by: Republic; Role: John Devlin

*Without Reservations*; Year released: 1946; Directed by: Mervyn LeRoy; Produced by: Jesse L. Lasky/RKO Radio; Role: Rusty Thomas

*Angel and the Badman*; Year released: 1947; Directed by: James Edward Grant; Produced by: John Wayne; Role: Quirt Evans

*Tycoon*; Year released: 1947; Directed by: Richard Wallace; Produced by: Stephen Ames/RKO Radio; Role: Johnny Munroe

*Fort Apache*; Year released: 1948; Directed by: John Ford; Produced by: John Ford-Merian Cooper/Argosy; Role: Captain Kirby York

*Red River*; Year released: 1948; Directed by: Howard Hawks; Produced by: Howard Hawks/Monterey; Role: Tom Dunson

*Three Godfathers*; Year released: 1949; Directed by: John Ford; Produced by: John Ford-Merian Cooper/Argosy; Role: Robert Hightower

*Wake of the Red Witch*; Year released: 1949; Directed by: Edward Ludwig; Produced by: Republic; Role: Captain Ralls

*The Fighting Kentuckian*; Year released: 1949; Directed by: George Waggner; Produced by: John Wayne/Republic; Role: John Breen

*She Wore a Yellow Ribbon*; Year released: 1949; Directed by: John Ford; Produced by: John Ford-Merian Cooper/Argosy; Role: Captain Nathan Brittles

*Sands of Iwo Jima*; Year released: 1949; Directed by: Allan Dwan; Produced by: Republic; Role: Sergeant John M. Stryker

*Rio Grande*; Year released: 1950; Directed by: John Ford; Produced by: John Ford-Merian Cooper/Argosy; Role: Lieutenant Colonel Kirby Yorke

*Operation Pacific*; Year released: 1951; Directed by: George Waggner; Produced by: Louis F. Edelman/Warner Bros.; Role: "Duke" Gifford

*Flying Leathernecks*; Year released: 1951; Directed by: Nicholas Ray; Produced by: Edmund Grainger/RKO Radio; Role: Major Dan Kirby

*The Quiet Man*; Year released: 1952; Directed by: John Ford; Produced by: John Ford-Merian Cooper/Argosy; Role: Sean Thornton

*Big Jim McLain*; Year released: 1952; Directed by: Edward Ludwig; Produced by: Robert Fellows/Wayne-Fellows; Role: Big Jim McLain

*Trouble Along the Way*; Year released: 1953; Directed by: Michael Curtiz; Produced by: Melville Shavelson/Warner Bros.; Role: Steve Williams

*Island in the Sky*; Year released: 1953; Directed by: William A. Wellman; Produced by: Robert Fellows/Wayne-Fellows; Role: Captain Dooley

*Hondo*; Year released: 1953; Directed by: John Farrow; Produced by: Robert Fellows/Wayne-Fellows; Role: Hondo Lane

*The High and Mighty*; Year released: 1954; Directed by: William A. Wellman; Produced by: Robert Fellows/Wayne-Fellows; Role: Dan Roman

*The Sea Chase*; Year released: 1955; Directed by: William A. Wellman; Produced by: John Farrow/Warner Bros.; Role: Captain Karl Ehrlich

*Blood Alley*; Year released: 1955; Directed by: William A. Wellman; Produced by: Batjac; Role: Wilder

*The Conqueror*; Year released: 1956; Directed by: Dick Powell; Produced by: Dick Powell/RKO Radio (Howard Hughes); Role: Temujin (Genghis Khan)

*The Searchers*; Year released: 1956; Directed by: John Ford; Produced by: Merian Cooper-C. V. Whitney/C. V. Whitney; Role: Ethan Edwards

*The Wings of Eagles*; Year released: 1957; Directed by: John Ford; Produced by: Charles Schnee/M-G-M; Role: Frank W. "Spig" Wead

*Jet Pilot*; Year released: 1957; Directed by: Josef von Sternberg; Produced by: Howard Hughes/RKO Radio; Role: Colonel Shannon

*Legend of the Lost*; Year released: 1957; Directed by: Henry Hathaway; Produced by: Henry Hathaway/Batjac/Robert Hagging/Dear Film; Role: Joe January

*I Married a Woman*; Year released: 1958; Directed by: Hal Kanter; Produced by: William Bloom/Universal-International (for RKO); Role: Himself

*The Barbarian and the Geisha*; Year released: 1958; Directed by: John Huston; Produced by: Eugene Frenke/20th-Century Fox; Role: Townsend Harris

*Rio Bravo*; Year released: 1959; Directed by: Howard Hawks; Produced by: Howard Hawks/Armada; Role: John T. Chance

*The Horse Soldiers*; Year released: 1959; Directed by: John Ford; Produced by: John Lee Mahin and Martin Rackin/Mahin-Rackin/Mirisch; Role: Colonel John Marlowe

*The Alamo*; Year released: 1960; Directed by: John Wayne; Produced by: John Wayne/Batjac; Role: Colonel David Crockett

*North to Alaska*; Year released: 1960; Directed by: Henry Hathaway; Produced by: Henry Hathaway; Role: Sam McCord

*The Comancheros*; Year released: 1961; Directed by: Michael Curtiz, John Wayne (uncredited); Produced by: George Sherman; Role: Jake Cutter

*The Man Who Shot Liberty Valance*; Year released: 1962; Directed by: John Ford; Produced by: Willis Goldbeck/John Ford Prods.; Role: Tom Doniphon

*Hatari!*; Year released: 1962; Directed by: Howard Hawks; Produced by: Howard Hawks/Malabar; Role: Sean Mercer

*How the West Was Won*; Year released: 1962; Directed by: John Ford/Henry Hathaway/Richard Thorpe (uncredited); Produced by: Bernard Smith; Role: General William T. Sherman

*Donovan's Reef*; Year released: 1963; Directed by: John Ford; Produced by: John Ford Prods.; Role: Michael Patrick Donovan

*The Longest Day*; Year released: 1963; Directed by: Ken Annakin/Andrew Marton/Bernhard Wicki/ Darryl F. Zanuck/Gerd Oswald; Produced by: Darryl F. Zanuck; Role: Lieutenant Colonel Benjamin Vandervoort

*McLintock!*; Year released: 1963; Directed by: Andrew V. McLaglen; Produced by: Michael Wayne/Batjac; Role: George Washington McLintock

*Circus World*; Year released: 1964; Directed by: Henry Hathaway;
  Produced by: Samuel Bronston/Bronston-Midway; Role: Matt
  Masters
*The Greatest Story Ever Told*; Year released: 1965; Directed by:
  George Stevens; Produced by: George Stevens; Role: The
  Centurion
*In Harm's Way*; Year released: 1965; Directed by: Otto Preminger;
  Produced by: Otto Preminger/Sigma; Role: Captain Rockwell
  Torrey
*The Sons of Katie Elder*; Year released: 1965; Directed by: Henry
  Hathaway; Produced by: Hal Wallis; Role: John Elder
*Cast a Giant Shadow*; Year released: 1966; Directed by: Melville
  Shavelson; Produced by: Melville Shavelson-Michael
  Wayne/Mirisch-Llenroc-Batjac; Role: General Mike Ran-
  dolph
*The War Wagon*; Year released: 1967; Directed by: Burt Kennedy;
  Produced by: Marvin Schwartz-Marvin Schwartz/Batjac;
  Role: Taw Jackson
*El Dorado*; Year released: 1967; Directed by: Howard Hawks; Pro-
  duced by: Howard Hawks/Laurel; Role: Cole Thornton
*The Green Berets*; Year released: 1968; Directed by: John Wayne and
  Ray Kellogg; Produced by: Michael Wayne/Batjac; Role:
  Colonel Mike Kirby
*Hellfighters*; Year released: 1969; Directed by: Andrew V.
  McLaglen; Produced by: Robert Arthur/Universal; Role:
  Chance Buckman
*True Grit*; Year released: 1969; Directed by: Henry Hathaway; Pro-
  duced by: Hal Wallis; Role: Reuben J. "Rooster" Cogburn
*The Undefeated*; Year released: 1969; Directed by: Andrew V.
  McLaglen; Produced by: Robert L. Jacks/20th-Century Fox;
  Role: Colonel John Henry Thomas
*Chisum*; Year released: 1970; Directed by: Andrew V. McLaglen;
  Produced by: Michael Wayne/Batjac; Role: John Chisum
*Rio Lobo*; Year released: 1970; Directed by: Howard Hawks; Pro-
  duced by: Howard Hawks/Malabar; Role: Cord McNally
*Big Jake*; Year released: 1971; Directed by: George Sherman; Pro-
  duced by: Michael Wayne/Batjac; Role: Jacob McCandles
*The Cowboys*; Year released: 1972; Directed by: Mark Rydell; Pro-
  duced by: Mark Rydell/Sanford; Role: Wil Andersen

*The Train Robbers*; Year released: 1973; Directed by: Burt Kennedy; Produced by: Michael Wayne/Batjac; Role: Lane

*Cahill: United States Marshall*; Year released: 1973; Directed by: Andrew V. McLaglen; Produced by: Michael Wayne/Batjac; Role: J. D. Cahill

*McQ*; Year released: 1974; Directed by: John Sturges; Produced by: Batjac/Levy-Gardner; Role: Det. Lieutenant Lon McQ

*Brannigan*; Year released: 1975; Directed by: Douglas Hickox; Produced by: Jules Levy-Arthur Gardner/Wellborn; Role: Brannigan

*Rooster Cogburn*; Year released: 1975; Directed by: Stuart Millar; Produced by: Hal B. Wallis; Role: Rooster Cogburn

*The Shootist*; Year released: 1976; Directed by: Don Siegel; Produced by: M. J. Francovich-William Self/Dino De Laurentis; Role: John Bernard Books

# APPENDIX B:
# CHRONOLOGY OF LIFE
# AND CAREER

| | |
|---|---|
| May 26, 1907 | Born in Winterset, Iowa |
| 1914 | Family moves to California |
| 1925-27 | Attends USC on football scholarship |
| 1926 | Summer work at Fox Studios; meets John Ford. |
| 1926-1930 | First screen appearances as double, extra, and in small roles |
| 1930 | First starring role, *The Big Trail*; signs five-year $75-a-week contract with Fox; renamed "John Wayne" |
| 1931 | Dropped by Fox; picked up by Columbia |
| 1932 | Dropped by Columbia |
| 1932-1939 | Makes over seventy films, most B westerns, under contract to Mascot, Warner's, Monogram, Universal, and Republic |
| June 24, 1933 | Marries Josephine Saenz after seven-year courtship |
| 1934 | First child, Michael, born |
| 1936 | Second child, Antonia Maria, born |
| 1937 | Third child, Patrick, born |
| 1939 | Emerges as a star in Ford's *Stagecoach* |

| | |
|---|---|
| 1939 | Fourth child, Melinda, born |
| 1940-1948 | Builds solid career as star in twenty-six films |
| 1942 | Signs new contract with Republic for 10% of gross and salary of $100,000 |
| 1944 | Visits American troops in New Guinea (family and age exempt him from WW II services). |
| December 26, 1945 | Divorced by Josephine Saenz |
| January 18, 1946 | Marries Esperanza ("Chata") Baur, Mexican actress |
| 1946 | Signs new contract with Republic which limits work to one high-budget film a year and allows him to produce films. Also contracts with RKO-Radio. |
| 1947 | Produces first film, *Angel and the Badman* |
| 1948 | After a series of mediocre films, makes *Fort Apache*; sets career in new direction of mature roles (*Red River*—1948, *She Wore a Yellow Ribbon*—1949, *Rio Grande*—1950) |
| 1949 | Elected to first of three terms as president of Motion Picture Alliance for the Preservation of American Ideals |
| 1949 | Nominated for Oscar as Best Actor for *Sands of Iwo Jima* |
| 1949-1960 | Appears in twenty-five films |
| 1949-1973 | Peak period of box office popularity; among "Top Ten Stars" in poll of film exhibitors every year except 1958. |
| 1951 | Forms Wayne-Fellows production company (later Batjac Production) |
| 1952 | Role in *The Quiet Man* for John Ford |
| 1952 | *Big Jim McLain*, first Wayne-Fellows production |
| November 1953 | Divorce trial creates scandal; divorced from Esperanza |
| November 1, 1954 | Marries Pilar Palette, Peruvian actress |

| | |
|---|---|
| 1956 | Three-picture, $2 million contract with 20th Century-Fox makes him highest salaried actor in history to date |
| 1956 | Role in *The Searchers* for John Ford |
| 1956 | Fifth child, Aissa, born |
| 1959 | Role in *Rio Bravo* for Howard Hawks |
| 1959-1960 | Produces, directs, stars in *The Alamo*, which costs his fortune and is nominated for twelve Academy Awards, winning Best Sound. |
| 1960-1976 | Appears in twenty-eight films |
| 1961 | Multipicture contract with Paramount pays $6 million in advance; cameo role in *The Longest Day* pays $200,000 |
| 1962 | Sixth child, Ethan, born |
| September 16, 1964 | Cancerous lung removed |
| 1966 | Visits troops in Vietnam |
| 1967 | Seventh child, Marissa, born |
| 1967-1968 | Produces, directs, stars in *The Green Berets* |
| 1968 | Addresses Republican National Convention |
| 1968 | Paid $1,000,000 by Universal for *Hellfighters* |
| 1969 | Performance in *True Grit* earns him Academy Award as Best Actor |
| 1973 | Separated from wife, Pilar |
| 1976 | Last film, *The Shootist* (Don Siegel) |
| March 1978 | Undergoes heart surgery |
| January 1979 | Gallbladder surgery; removal of cancerous stomach |
| April 1979 | Presents Academy Award for Best Picture; last public appearance |
| June 11, 1979 | Dies at UCLA Medical Center |
| March 6, 1980 | Congressional medal struck honoring "John Wayne—American" |
| June 9, 1980 | Awarded Presidential Medal of Freedom posthumously |

# INDEX

## ABOUT THE AUTHOR

JUDITH M. RIGGIN is Professor of English at Northern Virginia Community College, Annandale, Virginia.

**Recent Titles in
Popular Culture Bio-Bibliographies**

Charlie Chaplin: A Bio-Bibliography
*Wes D. Gehring*

Hank Williams: A Bio-Bibliography
*George William Koon*

Will Rogers: A Bio-Bibliography
*Peter C. Rollins*

Billy the Kid: A Bio-Bibliography
*Jon Tuska*

Errol Flynn: A Bio-Bibliography
*Peter Valenti*

W. C. Fields: A Bio-Bibliography
*Wes D. Gehring*

Elvis Presley: A Bio-Bibliography
*Pasty Guy Hammontree*

Charles A. Lindbergh: A Bio-Bibliography
*Perry D. Luckett*

The Marx Brothers: A Bio-Bibliography
*Wes D. Gehring*

Mae West: A Bio-Bibliography
*Carol M. Ward*

The Beatles: A Bio-Bibliography
*William McKeen*

Laurel & Hardy: A Bio-Bibliography
*Wes D. Gehring*